REEDS
MARINE
DECK

COLLISION
REGULATIONS
HANDBOOK

REEDS
MARINE
DECK

COLLISION
REGULATIONS
HANDBOOK

SIMON JINKS

REEDS
LONDON · OXFORD · NEW YORK · NEW DELHI · SYDNEY

The author would like to thank Captain Jerry Webster for his help and ideas in compiling this book.

REEDS
Bloomsbury Publishing Plc
50 Bedford Square, London, WC1B 3DP, UK
29 Earlsfort Terrace, Dublin 2, Ireland

BLOOMSBURY, REEDS, and the Reeds logo are trademarks of Bloomsbury Publishing Plc

First published in Great Britain 2023
Copyright © Simon Jinks, 2022
Illustrations © Dave Saunders, 2022
Images © Getty, with the exception of: pv, p20 © Shutterstock; p19 © Ali Khara; p64 © Adobe Stock; p76 © Julie Proudfoot; p100 © Steenbergs/Wikimedia; p102 © Paul Hudson/Wikimedia

Simon Jinks has asserted his right under the Copyright, Designs and Patents Act, 1988, to be identified as Author of this work

Contains public sector information licensed under the Open Government Licence v3.0
Active Marine Guidance Notices (MGNs) have been reproduced from the Maritime and Coastguard Agency
For legal purposes the sources on p208 constitute an extension of this copyright page

All rights reserved. No part of this publication may be reproduced or transmitted in any form or by any means, electronic or mechanical, including photocopying, recording, or any information storage or retrieval system, without prior permission in writing from the publishers

Bloomsbury Publishing Plc does not have any control over, or responsibility for, any third-party websites referred to or in this book. All internet addresses given in this book were correct at the time of going to press. The author and publisher regret any inconvenience caused if addresses have changed or sites have ceased to exist, but can accept no responsibility for any such changes

While all reasonable care has been taken in the publication of this book, the publisher takes no responsibility for the use of the methods or products described in the book.

A catalogue record for this book is available from the British Library

Library of Congress Cataloguing-in-Publication data has been applied for

ISBN: PB: 978-1-3994-0221-7; ePub: 978-1-3994-0222-4; ePDF: 9781—3994-0223-1

2 4 6 8 10 9 7 5 3 1

Typeset in Roboto by Nick Avery Design

Printed and bound in India by Replika Press Pvt Ltd

To find out more about our authors and books visit www.bloomsbury.com and sign up for our newsletters

Understanding the Collision Regulations

Rules for avoiding collision at sea have been about for many years. The earliest recorded were understandably for vessels under sail. Admiral Lord Richard Howe in the 1770s noted: 'In order to avoid inconvenience from the customary practice with respect to the conduct of Senior Officers towards their juniors, ships of war are to bear up for each other, shorten sail, etc, without regard to the seniority of the Commanders or other claims of distinction... But when ships  are upon different tacks and must come near each other, the ship on the starboard tack is to keep her wind while that on the larboard (port) tack is always to pass to leeward.' Interestingly, the essence of this rule is still in force today – although written a little differently.

Some of the first statutory rules for British Ships on collision avoidance were those laid down by Trinity House in London in the 1840s, resulting in the Steam Navigation Act of 1846. This called for steam vessels to pass port to port and stay on the starboard side of the channel. It also required vessels to be lit at night when within 20 miles of the coast. Up until then, most laws were specific to local rivers. Rules changed slowly over the years; the greatest change, once the primary rules were set, was with the advent of radar.

The rules we use today, The International Regulations for the Prevention of Collision at Sea, were adopted in 1972 and amended over time. They are published by the International Maritime Organization (IMO) and then adopted by each country or flag state worldwide.

The regulations are not very long, but they use particular words and phrases for describing vessels in particular circumstances at sea and this book hopes to assist by explaining their meaning and how they are applied.

This book is to assist those who need to have a deeper knowledge of the collision regulations at sea. It is set out so that the rule is quoted, followed by my explanation of the rule (in yellow boxes). It should be noted that there are always exceptions to a rule and many different interpretations. Sometimes it is just down to the particular situation or, as the rules often state, 'if the circumstances of the case admit'.

Contents

		Rules	Page
PART A	GENERAL	1–3	11
PART B	STEERING AND SAILING RULES	4–19	21
	Section I – Conduct of vessels in any conditions of visibility	4–10	21
	Section II – Conduct of vessels in sight of one another	11–18	43
	Section III – Conduct of vessels in restricted visibility	19	59
PART C	LIGHTS AND SHAPES	20–31	65
PART D	SOUND AND LIGHT SIGNALS	32–37	91
PART E	EXEMPTIONS	38	99
PART F	VERIFICATION OF COMPLIANCE	39–41	101
ANNEX I	POSITIONING AND TECHNICAL DETAILS OF LIGHTS AND SHAPES		103
ANNEX II	ADDITIONAL SIGNALS FOR FISHING VESSELS FISHING IN CLOSE PROXIMITY		113
ANNEX III	TECHNICAL DETAILS OF SOUND SIGNAL APPLIANCES		115
ANNEX IV	DISTRESS SIGNALS		119

	Page
Watchkeeping	121
Exam preparation	128
Radar and basic plotting	131
Questions	142
Appendices	
MGN 324 Operational guidance on the use of VHF radio and Automatic Identification Systems at sea	170
MGN 364 Traffic separation schemes – application of Rule 10 and navigation in the Dover Strait	176
MGN 369 Navigation in restricted visibility	182
MGN 379 Use of electronic navigation aids	191
Index	206

Contents explained

Understanding the contents page can really simplify the Collision Regulations. The contents page identifies when particular parts or sections of the rules apply. The rules are often written in a 'seemingly' legal language, so it takes time to know what they mean. For instance:

Rule 13(a) Overtaking: 'Notwithstanding anything contained in the Rules of Part B, Sections I and II, any vessel overtaking any other shall keep out of the way of the vessel being overtaken.'

To decipher what this sentence actually means we need to know: What is a 'part' and what are the 'sections'?

Abbreviations

Throughout the text the following abbreviations may be used:

COLREGS or IRPCS	Collision Regulations – International Regulation for Prevention of Collisions at Sea
PDV	Power-driven vessel
PDV under 20m	Power-driven vessel under 20m in length
Sail	Sailing vessel (under sail, not power)
VEF	Vessel engaged in fishing
RAM	Restricted in ability to manoeuvre
CBD	Constrained by draught
NUC	Not under command
WIG	Wing in Ground craft
TSS	Traffic Separation Scheme
ITZ	Inshore Traffic Zone
IMO	International Maritime Organization
SOLAS	Safety of Lives at Sea Convention
STCW	Standards of Training, Certification and Watchkeeping
MSN	Merchant Shipping Notice
MGN	Marine Guidance Note
MIN	Marine Information Note

The COLREGS are made up of six parts, three sections and four annexes:

Parts

Part A – General		
Rules 1–3	These rules apply at all times and include how they apply (1), the responsibility of the Master and crew (2) and any specific definitions (3).	
Part B – General		
Rules 4–19	Part B actually tells us what to do, and what NOT to do if a risk of collision or close-quarters situation exists. However, Part B, the Steering and Sailing Rules, is divided into three sections and these inform us when a particular set of rules apply and when they don't:	
	Section I (Rules 4–10)	Conduct of vessels in any conditions of visibility	**APPLY AT ALL TIMES.** When we look at these rules, many concern how we actually run the bridge and the vessel: how to keep a look-out (5), operate at a safe speed (6), establish a risk of collision (7) and how to act if there is a risk of collision (8), etc.
	Section II (Rules 11–18)	Conduct of vessels in sight of one another	**These rules only apply if we are IN SIGHT of the other vessel.** These include: sailing vessels (12), overtaking (13), head-on (14), crossing situations (15), stand-on (16), give-way (17) and priority of vessels (18). But we would only use these rules and the rules of Section I if we were IN SIGHT of the other vessel.
	Section III (Rule 19)	Conduct of vessels in restricted visibility	**This rule only applies if we are IN RESTRICTED VISIBILITY.** In restricted visibility we would use the rules in Section I (4–10) and Section III (19). But we would not use the rules in Section II (11–18).
			This is why there is no stand-on or give-way vessel in restricted visibility. In restricted visibility, rule 19 gives us everything we need to know about what we would need to do when vessels are coming from different angles towards our vessel, and the rules of Section I give us greater knowledge about how to conduct our vessel in restricted visibility.
	All three sections concern whether there is visibility and whether we are in sight of one another.		

Parts C, D, E and F, and the Annexes speak for themselves, although it is worth bearing in mind that Annex IV contains Distress Signals.

PART A – GENERAL

Rule 1

Application

(a) These Rules shall apply to all vessels upon the high seas and in all waters connected therewith navigable by seagoing vessels.

> The pertinent words here are 'all vessels' and 'upon the high seas and in all waters connected therewith'. In general terms, the collision regulations apply at all times as mostly all vessels are on stretches of water that are either high seas or connected with them, such as rivers and estuaries. However, there is a possibility that they might not apply on some inland lakes; although precedent and simplicity normally mean that they are also adopted here.
> On the North American Great Lakes, the rules apply but with significant modifications. For instance, they include many mentions of 'right of way', whereas the standard Collision Regulations make no mention of a vessel having any 'right of way' over another. All vessels have a responsibility to avoid a collision.
> In most of continental Europe, the European Code for Navigation on Inland Waters (CEVNI) applies, which significantly modifies the rules.
> Therefore, there are places where the COLREGS may not apply, but in general terms, if the waters join the sea – then they do.

(b) Nothing in these Rules shall interfere with the operation of special rules made by an appropriate authority for roadsteads, harbours, rivers, lakes or inland waterways connected with the high seas and navigable by seagoing vessels. Such special rules shall conform as closely as possible to these Rules.

> For instance, the Port of London Authority (PLA) and other ports adapt the regulations and sound signals. The PLA Thames Byelaws have modifications to

PART 4

STEERING AND SAILING BYELAWS

23. OBLIGATION OF THE MASTER
It is the duty of the master of a vessel to comply with the requirements of this Part of these byelaws.

24. MODIFICATIONS TO THE INTERNATIONAL COLLISION REGULATIONS
Notwithstanding Part C of the International Collision Regulations and Annex I:
a) a vessel must not cross or enter a fairway so as to obstruct another vessel proceeding along the fairway;
b) when a power-driven vessel operating as a ferry is crossing the fairway, it must keep out of the way of a vessel proceeding along the fairway;
c) a power-driven vessel must not proceed abreast of another power-driven vessel except for the purposes of overtaking that other vessel; and
d) a vessel in a fairway above Tilburyness must not overtake a vessel which is itself overtaking another vessel
e) all vessels must, in determining a safe speed, have regard to:
   i) the safety of other river users, passengers and crew,
   ii) tidal flow, and
   iii) the navigational environment including port infrastructure.

Note: The steering and sailing rules in byelaw 24 are inconsistent with the provisions of the International Collision Regulations but apply as special rules by virtue of rule 1(b) as applied by the Merchant Shipping (Distress Signals and Prevention of Collisions) Regulation 1996. It is the duty of the master of a vessel to comply with the requirements of the International Collision Regulations except as provided for in Byelaw 24.

▲ Excerpt: Port of London Thames Byelaws Rule 1(b)

Steering and Sailing Rules, Lights and Shapes and Sound Signals where they adapt or modify a COLREG to mean something similar but more suited to the Thames, such as sound signals for 'turning about' (doing a 180-degree course change).

(c) Nothing in these Rules shall interfere with the operation of any special rules made by the Government of any State with respect to additional station or signal lights, shapes or whistle signals for ships of war and vessels proceeding under convoy, or with respect to additional station or signal lights or shapes for fishing vessels engaged in fishing as a fleet. These additional station or signal lights, shapes or whistle signals shall, so far as possible, be such that they cannot be mistaken for any light, shape or signal authorised elsewhere under these Rules.

PART A – GENERAL

> Examples of this modification: *The Mariner's Handbook* states that some submarines may exhibit a very quick flashing yellow (amber) light. In the US, the Code of Federal Regulations states: 'Submarines may display, as a distinctive means of identification, an intermittent flashing amber (yellow) beacon with a sequence of one flash per second for three (3) seconds followed by a three (3) second off-period. Other special rules made by the Secretary of the Navy with respect to additional station and signal lights are found in Part 706 of Title 32, Code of Federal Regulations (32 CFR 706).' Further details can be found in *The Mariner's Handbook*.

(d) Traffic separation schemes may be adopted by the Organization for the purpose of these Rules.

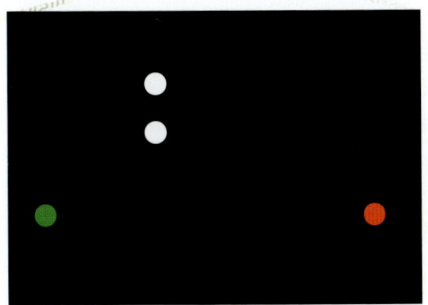

▲ Rule 1(e). Sometimes aircraft carrier lights may need to be offset by necessity

> In this context, Organization means International Maritime Organization.

(e) Whenever the Government concerned shall have determined that a vessel of any special construction or purpose cannot comply with the provisions of any of these Rules with respect to the number, position, range or arc of visibility of lights or shapes, as well as to the disposition and characteristics of sound-signalling appliances, such vessel shall comply with such other provisions in regard to the number, position, range or arc of visibility of lights or shapes, as well as to the disposition and characteristics of sound-signalling appliances, as her Government shall have determined to be the closest possible compliance with these Rules in respect of that vessel.

> **Rule 1(e)** allows a Government to change the positioning of equipment such as lights; for example, Rule 21 'Definitions' states that masthead lights shall be placed fore and aft over the centreline of the vessel – an aircraft carrier might offset the lights to allow space for the flight deck.
> It also states that it shall still comply as closely as possible to the rule.

Rule 2

Responsibility

(a) Nothing in these Rules shall exonerate any vessel, or the owner, Master or crew thereof, from the consequences of any neglect to comply with these Rules or of the neglect of any precaution which may be required by the ordinary practice of seamen, or by the special circumstances of the case.

> This addresses not only the Master, but the owner, Master or crew or the total sum of those in control of the 'Vessel'. This also encompasses autonomous surface vessels and their background controllers ashore. Therefore, there is no reason you can use for not complying with the rules.
>
> The 'ordinary practice of seamen' could be summed up by complying with Collision Regulations, bridge watchkeeping regulations, keeping a look-out, maintaining a log, following Master's orders, etc. For instance, a key 'Master's Standing Order' would be to 'call the Master' if an officer of the watch is unsure of a situation.
>
> This 'neglect' is not only by our own ship, but also neglect by other vessels. So, your own ship is not exonerated if your ship has a collision because the other vessel did not follow the rules. This is why all ships have a responsibility to avoid a collision and if a collision does occur, the courts will often apportion a percentage of blame to each party.
>
> The owner is not exempt from the rules, as they should ensure that vessels have the correct manning, trained and rested persons and equipment on board (including lights, shapes, sound signals) so the vessel can comply with the ColRegs. Their Safety Management System (SMS) should include audit procedures to ensure that ColRegs are followed.
>
> - The definition of Master and Seaman from Merchant Shipping Act S. 313: 'Master' includes every person (except a pilot) having command or charge of a ship and, in relation to a fishing vessel, means the skipper; 'seaman' includes every person (except Masters and pilots) employed or engaged in any capacity on board any ship.

(b) In construing and complying with these Rules due regard shall be had to all dangers of navigation and collision and to any special circumstances, including the limitations of the vessels involved, which may make a departure from these Rules necessary to avoid immediate danger.

Rule 2(b) conjures up the words of Shakespeare 'to be or not to be' or in our case, 2(b) or not 2(b)... Whether we can use Rule 2(b), and when we can 'make a departure from the rules necessary to avoid immediate danger'. Many situations at sea are not clear-cut. Most collision regulations are written where one vessel meets one other vessel in clear open sea, where there are no navigational hazards to avoid. However, life is rarely like that and a conventional turn may not be possible because of another vessel hindering our turn or our proximity to a navigational hazard.

Therefore, we always 'follow the rules', but we may have to make a departure from the quoted text 'to avoid immediate danger', because of a particular set of circumstances.

In deciding whether this is allowable, we must take into account not just our vessel but the *limitations of the other vessels* involved, or the proximity of other hazards. It might mean that one or both of the vessels cannot take the normal action because of the actions of other vessels, or a navigational danger hampering our manoeuvre.

By summing up Rule 2, it puts a responsibility on everybody and every vessel to avoid a collision, whether complying with the letter of the ColRegs (2a) or making a departure from them (2b).

A departure from these rules may be required owing to dangers of navigation or to dangers of collision. For example, in a head-on situation, one vessel may be unable to alter to starboard due to the presence of shallow water on that side, or due to the presence of a third vessel.

A departure is only permitted when there are special circumstances AND immediate danger. BOTH CONDITIONS MUST APPLY.

Rule 2(a) says that we *must* COMPLY with the Rules; 2(b) says we *must* make a DEPARTURE from them if necessary to avoid collision in special circumstances and to avoid immediate danger!

Making a rare departure from is, therefore, still in compliance with the rules.

When formulating the rules, the rule makers were aware that there are many instances when a pragmatic approach is necessary, and that is why the Collision Regulations are littered with the following clauses:

- if the circumstances of the case admit;
- when required by the circumstances of the case;
- as safe as practicable.

If you are using Rule 2b and making a departure from the rules, Rule 8 should be taken into account and the manoeuvre must be 'positive', 'made in ample time', 'with due regard to good seamanship', 'result in passing at a safe distance', etc.

Rule 3

General definitions

For the purpose of these Rules, except where the context otherwise requires:

(a) The word 'vessel' includes every description of water craft, including non-displacement craft, WIG craft and seaplanes, used or capable of being used as a means of transportation on water.

> For the most part, the definition of a vessel is all inclusive. However, in the UK there is a precedent set where a Personal Water Craft (PWC) was judged to be 'not a ship and not used in navigation' and, therefore, the Merchant Shipping Act and COLREGS would not apply to them. This judgement came about after a collision in Weymouth in England (R v Goodwin, 2005). In the UK, the Maritime and Coastguard Agency and Royal Yachting Association have issued statements that PWCs and the like should follow ColRegs as best practice. Other countries, such as Australia, state that PWCs are included in the ColRegs. The UK Government is currently proposing changes to the laws regarding PWCs, to bring them more into line with those applicable to other boats and ships.

(b) The term 'power-driven vessel' means any vessel propelled by machinery.

> When reading the rules, there are many instances where rules apply solely to power-driven vessels and others are written for 'all vessels' or 'a vessel'. Care should be taken when reading the rules to check that the rule applies to the vessel you are operating. For instance, Rule 15 states: 'When two power-driven vessels are crossing...', therefore this would not apply if one of the vessels were not a power-driven vessel.
>
> Rowing boats are not mentioned in the definitions. They are normally considered PDVs and some harbour-byelaws have included them as such as the oar and the person combined is the machine.

(c) The term 'sailing vessel' means any vessel under sail provided that propelling machinery, if fitted, is not being used.

> If a sailing vessel has a sail hoisted and is being propelled by engine, she should show a day shape of a black cone apex downwards and would then be a power-driven vessel.

PART A – GENERAL

(d) The term 'vessel engaged in fishing' means any vessel fishing with nets, lines, trawls or other fishing apparatus which restrict manoeuvrability, but does not include a vessel fishing with trolling lines or other fishing apparatus which do not restrict manoeuvrability.

> Key term here is *engaged* in fishing. So, the vessel may look and smell like a fishing boat, but if she is not *engaged* in fishing, she is simply a power-driven vessel.
>
> The problem is that a fishing vessel often exhibits the lights or shapes of a vessel 'engaged in fishing' at all times, even when she is en route to a fishing ground or alongside on a quay, so it is a difficult rule to enforce at sea because by the time you are close enough to see if the vessel is engaged in fishing, you are probably too close to take early action. Rule 26(e) states that she should only show fishing lights and shapes when actually '*engaged* in fishing'.

(e) The word 'seaplane' includes any aircraft designed to manoeuvre on the water.

(f) The term 'vessel not under command' means a vessel which through some exceptional circumstance is unable to manoeuvre as required by these Rules and is therefore unable to keep out of the way of another vessel.

> Key term here is 'through some *exceptional* circumstance is *unable* to manoeuvre'. An exceptional circumstance could be rudder or main engine failure. Because it states 'a vessel', this could also mean a sailing boat that is becalmed or possibly 'hove-to' in a storm.

(g) The term 'vessel restricted in her ability to manoeuvre' means a vessel which from the nature of her work is restricted in her ability to manoeuvre as required by these Rules and is therefore unable to keep out of the way of another vessel. The term 'vessels restricted in their ability to manoeuvre' shall include but not be limited to:

> Key term here is 'a vessel which *from the nature of her work*' as opposed to the definition of Not Under Command above. The list of possible work natures is given below.

 (i) a vessel engaged in laying, servicing or picking up a navigation mark, submarine cable or pipeline;
 (ii) a vessel engaged in dredging, surveying or underwater operations;
 (iii) a vessel engaged in replenishment or transferring persons, provisions or cargo while underway;
 (iv) a vessel engaged in the launching or recovery of aircraft;
 (v) a vessel engaged in mine clearance operations;

(vi) a vessel engaged in a towing operation such as severely restricts the towing vessel and her tow in their ability to deviate from their course.

> Therefore, in the case of 3(g)(vi), a tow may not straight away mean that she is a Restricted in Ability to Manoeuvre (RAM) vessel. A tow at sea may be not RAM, but then as she closes the coast or constricted water, the vessel may decide to change her status to RAM because of the circumstances of the case.

(h) The term 'vessel constrained by her draught' means a power-driven vessel which, because of her draught in relation to the available depth and width of navigable water, is severely restricted in her ability to deviate from the course she is following.

> Note that this only refers to a 'power-driven vessel' and not a sailing vessel. However, a sailing yacht could use this definition so long as she was not being propelled by sails and was under engine power.
>
> When delving deeper into the rules, it is evident that a vessel constrained by her draught (CBD) remains a 'power-driven vessel' by definition, and other vessels should treat her as such in the Rules, although they should also avoid impeding her safe passage – see Rule 18(d).
>
> The word 'width' was added to deter vessels from displaying CBD signals (and hence gain privileges) when navigating in areas of limited under-keel clearance but where the depth is similar over large areas around the ship, for example, in the Dover Straits, where a vessel could still take action.

(i) The word 'underway' means that a vessel is not at anchor, or made fast to the shore, or aground.

> While underway is defined in Rule 3, the 'Lights and Sounds' sections in ColRegs discusses 'Underway' and 'Making Way'. Making way is not defined here, but would be surmised as when the vessel is in gear and making way through the water.
>
> Rules still apply if you are underway and stopped: for instance, if you are underway and pleasure fishing and drifting with the tide and wind, you will still be a give-way vessel if a vessel is approaching on your starboard side in a crossing situation (Rule 15).

(j) The words 'length' and 'breadth' of a vessel mean her length overall and greatest breadth.

PART A – GENERAL

> These definitions usually come into play with lights and shapes and sound signals, where vessels of different sizes show or sound different signals. They also apply in Rules 9(b) and 10(j), Narrow Channels and Traffic Separation Schemes.

(k) Vessels shall be deemed to be in sight of one another only when one can be observed visually from the other.

> This is an important definition as the Sections within Part B of the ColRegs are:
>
> - Section I – Conduct of vessels in any conditions of visibility
> - Section II – Conduct of vessels *in sight* of one another
> - Section III – Conduct of vessels in restricted visibility.
>
> Visually would be by sight using eyes, but not radar when not in visual sight.

(l) The term 'restricted visibility' means any condition in which visibility is restricted by fog, mist, falling snow, heavy rainstorms, sandstorms or any other similar causes.

> Other similar causes could be smoke from land or vessels. It does not mean a vessel is obscured by landmass or other vessels.

(m) The term 'Wing-in-Ground (WIG) craft' means a multimodal craft which, in its main operational mode, flies in close proximity to the surface by utilizing surface-effect action.

> WIGs are similar to aircraft in design, but travel at very low height riding a cushion of air between the lower wing and sea surface.

▲ Rule 3(m). Wing-in-Ground (WIG) Craft

PART B – Steering and Sailing Rules

SECTION I – Conduct of vessels in any condition of visibility

Rule 4

Application

Rules in this Section apply in any condition of visibility.

> Rules in Section 1 give a good idea of how a vessel's bridge should be run. For instance, look-outs should be posted, a safe speed should be adhered to, look-outs and officers briefed on how to establish a risk of collision and what equipment to use in doing so. All solid parts of bridge watchkeeping.
> Whatever the state of the visibility, as soon as you go out on any water, Rules 5–10 apply at all times, where applicable.
> Rules in this section cover the basics of good seamanship; they emphasise actions to avoid the risk of collision developing, rather than dictating action to take once that risk exists.

Rule 5

Look-out

Every vessel shall at all times maintain a proper look-out by sight and hearing as well as by all available means

Rule 5 ▶

appropriate in the prevailing circumstances and conditions so as to make a full appraisal of the situation and of the risk of collision.

> In Rule 5, the reason that a 'proper look-out' is kept is so that a 'full appraisal' of the situation can be made. 'Appraisal' usually means pulling information in from many different sources on which a decision can finally be made. Rule 7 states how we would use that information to 'determine' whether a risk of collision exists.
>
> The IMO STCW Code (Ch VIII) defines a look-out's three main responsibilities:
> 1. Maintaining a continuous state of vigilance by sight and hearing as well as by all other available means, with regard to any significant change in the operating environment;
> 2. Fully appraising the situation and the risk of collision, stranding and other dangers to navigation; and
> 3. Detecting ships or aircraft in distress, shipwrecked persons, wrecks, debris and other hazards to safe navigation.
>
> As well as sight and hearing, 'all available means' could include radar, AIS, echo sounder, VHF, compass, log, plotter/ECDIS and Navtex, because in Rule 5 we are 'appraising' the situation, therefore pulling in all the information. In Rule 7 we are then 'determining' whether a risk of collision exists, therefore, the information used will be more definite. The responsibilities of a look-out are discussed in 'Watchkeeping' (see page 124).

Rule 6

Safe speed

Every vessel shall at all times proceed at a safe speed so that she can take proper and effective action to avoid collision and be stopped within a distance appropriate to the prevailing circumstances and conditions.

> Every vessel 'shall at all times' means that there is always an obligation put upon the Master and Mate to maintain a safe speed. Why? 'So that she can take proper and effective action to avoid collision and be stopped within a distance appropriate to the prevailing circumstances and conditions.' A vessel may be unable to take proper and effective action due to the speed being too high or, in some circumstances, too low.

PART B – STEERING AND SAILING RULES

Rule 19(b) also states that 'every vessel shall proceed at a safe speed adapted to the prevailing circumstances and conditions of restricted visibility'. A power-driven vessel shall have her engines ready for immediate manoeuvre.

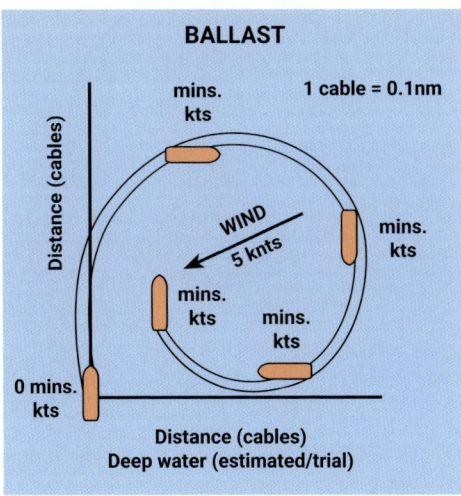

◀ Rule 6(a)(iii). Excerpt from a wheelhouse poster for the ships handling characteristics when in Ballast. The wheelhouse poster is a useful source of manoeuvring information

In determining a safe speed, the following factors shall be among those taken into account:

(a) By all vessels:
  (i) the state of visibility;
  (ii) the traffic density including concentrations of fishing vessels or any other vessels;
  (iii) the manoeuvrability of the vessel with special reference to stopping distance and turning ability in the prevailing conditions;

On a large vessel, manoeuvrability information may be gained from the 'Wheelhouse poster', which should give the manoeuvring information for the ship.

  (iv) at night the presence of background light such as from shore lights or from back scatter of her own lights;

Back scatter is the light reflection of the vessel's instruments on the windscreen or glare reflection of her nav lights on the vessel's superstructure.

(v) the state of wind, sea and current, and the proximity of navigational hazards;
(vi) the draught in relation to the available depth of water.

Two ways of remembering the six factors to safe speed are:
Clean version: **V**isibly **D**ense **M**an **S**catters **H**azards **D**eep.
Salty version: **VD M**akes **L**ittle **W**illies **D**roop (Visibility, Density, Manoeuvrability, Lights, Wind/weather, Draught).

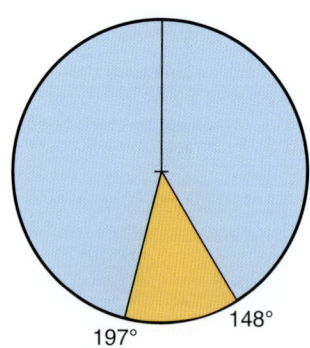

▲ Rule 6(b)(ii). RADAR blind arc poster on a ship to alert the watch keeper of possible blind areas (such as the ship's funnel or crane etc)

(b) Additionally, by vessels with operational radar:
(i) the characteristics, efficiency and limitations of the radar equipment;

This could include the radar's beam width, power, height of scanner, blind sectors, whether it operates on X or S Band and any limitations that may impose.

(ii) any constraints imposed by the radar range scale in use;

For instance, if you are using radar on a one-mile range a contact six miles away will not be seen, but if the closing speed is 20 knots, it will relatively travel two miles in six minutes.
   Remember to use different range scales, to range-out and range-in, so that situational awareness ahead and small objects are not missed.
   See also Rule 7(b) – long-range scanning.

(iii) the effect on radar detection of the sea state, weather and other sources of interference;

This can also work alongside Rule 6(b)(i), and take into account adjustment of sea

PART B – STEERING AND SAILING RULES

and rain clutter controls and the possibility that small objects may be lost, or large objects may reduce in size, if the clutter controls are incorrectly adjusted.

(iv) the possibility that small vessels, ice and other floating objects may not be detected by radar at an adequate range;

As many small vessels do not show up on radar because of their physical size or construction of wood or GRP, SOLAS (Chapter V, Regulation 19) requires small vessels under 150 GT to fit a radar reflector.

Used in conjunction with other rules such as Rule 6(a)(v) (Proximity of other hazards) and Rule 5 (Look-out) Maritime Safety Information from Navtex and radio warnings of containers, ice or debris should be taken into account.

(v) the number, location and movement of vessels detected by radar;

For instance, if there is a fishing fleet ahead, it may take much more time and situational awareness to establish the picture and approximate aspects using radar than it will using sight.

(vi) the more exact assessment of the visibility that may be possible when radar is used to determine the range of vessels or other objects in the vicinity.

Travelling through a bank of grey fog on a grey sea can give little idea of how much visibility there is because your depth of field and visual perception is affected. If a vessel is tracked on radar and then emerges from a fog bank ahead and is sighted visually, the radar range can be taken of the emerging vessel and the range of the vessel noted giving a good estimation of the actual visibility at sea.

Two ways of remembering the six factors of safe speed part B (radar) are:

1. CR WINE:
- **C**haracteristics
- **R**ange
- **W**eather
- **I**ce
- **N**umber
- **E**xact

2. Charlie's Cats Eat Pies No More:
- **C**haracteristics
- **C**onstraints
- **E**ffect on
- **P**ossibility that
- **N**umber
- **M**ore exact assessment

COLLISION REGULATIONS HANDBOOK

Rule 7

Risk of collision

(a) Every vessel shall use all available means appropriate to the prevailing circumstances and conditions to determine if risk of collision exists. If there is any doubt such risk shall be deemed to exist.

> 'All available means' is the same term as in Rule 5 (Look-out), but here it is to 'determine whether a risk of collision exists' instead of 'to make a full appraisal of the risk' as in Rule 5.
>
> When appraising, we may use many different forms of information to build a picture of what is happening. However, when determining, we would only use verifiable information – therefore sight, hearing and radar as it is our eyes, ears and radar gaining the information.
>
> Information from AIS and VHF would be treated with great caution and not relied on to 'determine a risk of collision', as AIS information is plotting a theoretical GPS position sent by another party and may be wrong, VHF information communication might be with a different vessel to the one you think it is. MGN 324 (in the Annex) suggests that over-reliance could lead to breaching Rule 7(c): 'Assumptions shall not be based on scanty information'.

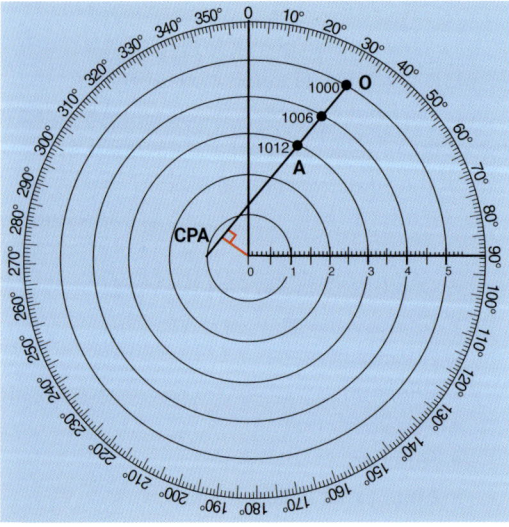

◄ Rule 7(b). Systematic plotting of a target or ARPA/MARPA use

PART B – STEERING AND SAILING RULES

(b) Proper use shall be made of radar equipment if fitted and operational, including long-range scanning to obtain early warning of risk of collision and radar plotting or equivalent systematic observation of detected objects.

> 'Proper use' indicates that the radar is on, tuned and adjusted correctly, on the correct range scale and being monitored regularly by a competent operator. 'Long-range scanning' suggests that instead of staying on a short range if you are using the radar for pilotage, you regularly range out to see what is coming up on you.
>
> We will see in Rule 19 (Restricted visibility) that if a vessel is picked up by radar alone, certain duties are imposed; but these change when we hear a fog signal. We may hear a fog signal at a two-mile range (so say the technical specifications in Annex III), so collision avoidance solely using radar in restricted visibility might be considered when vessels are well over the two-mile audible range of the fog signal, once again indicating the need for long range scanning, especially as any action to avoid collision needs to be 'readily apparent to vessels with radar' (Rule 8(b)).
>
> 'Systematic plotting' refers to manual or automatic plotting such as ARPA/MARPA, monitoring the target with the EBL/VRM, or paper plotting to establish whether a risk exists. A single plot is not sufficient information as it is not a series of bearings.

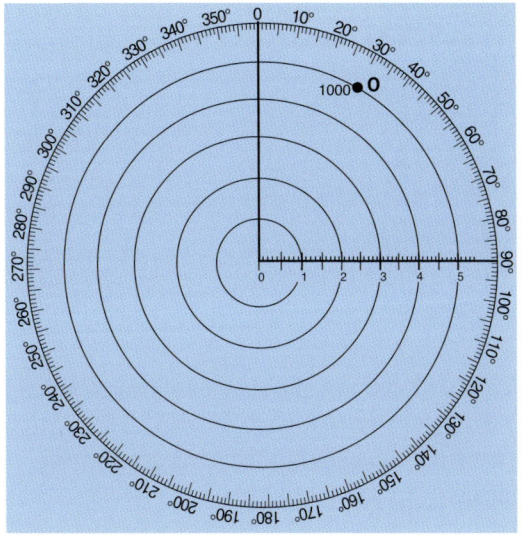

◀ Rule 7(c). Only one plot? It could be scanty 'information'. We require systematic observation, therefore a few plots, a trend over time using the EBL or enough time given to ARPA to correctly 'lock-on' before we can correctly 'determine' whether a risk exists

(c) Assumptions shall not be made on the basis of scanty information, especially scanty radar information.

SECTION I – Conduct of vessels in any condition of visibility **4–10**

If you only have one plot on the radar, it would be scanty information; however, 'systematic observation' – or a series of plots – would confirm the target's Closest Point of Approach (CPA). Don't jump to conclusions without first establishing what the vessel is doing over a period of time.

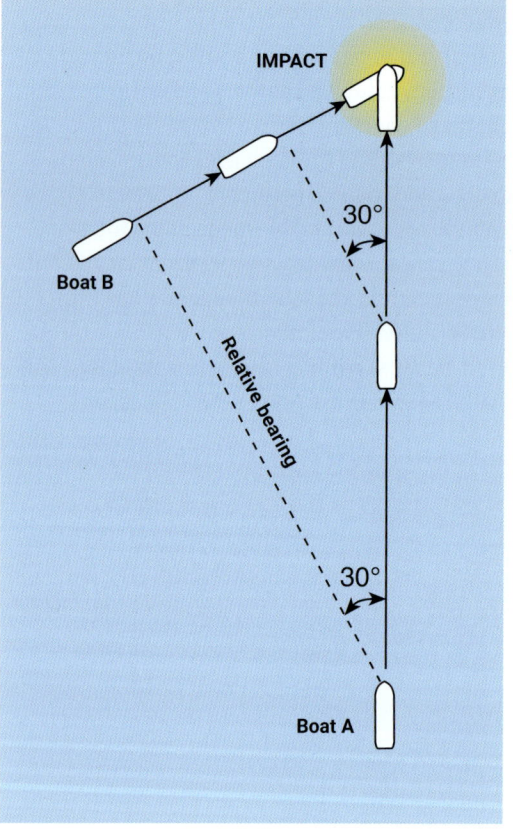

◀ Rule 7(d). Vessels on a constant bearing can lead to a collision

(d) In determining if risk of collision exists the following considerations shall be among those taken into account:
   (i) such risk shall be deemed to exist if the compass bearing of an approaching vessel does not appreciably change;

So, to decide whether we are on a collision course we would 'determine whether a risk of collision exists by taking a series of compass bearings to check if there is no appreciable change'.

PART B – STEERING AND SAILING RULES

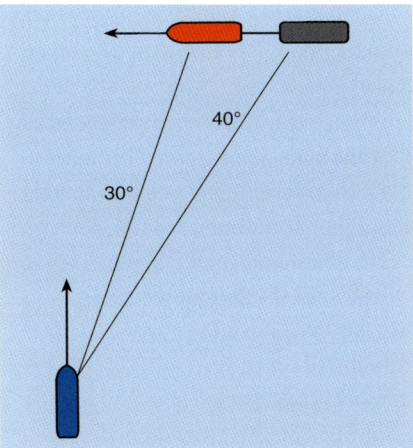

◄ Rule 7(d)(ii). While a constant bearing is the best method of establishing a risk of collision, it is not infallible. Tugs and tows, small alterations of one of the vessels can all alter bearings, but still lead to a collision

(ii) such risk may sometimes exist even when an appreciable bearing change is evident, particularly when approaching a very large vessel or a tow or when approaching a vessel at close range.

> Because you may be looking at a different part of the vessel when taking each bearing, or you may miss the tug, but hit the tow, etc. Or because the approaching vessel may be making a series of small alterations contrary to the rules: 'Such risk may sometimes exist even when an appreciable bearing change is evident.'

Rule 8

Action to avoid collision

(a) Any action taken to avoid collision shall be taken in accordance with the Rules of this Part and shall, if the circumstances of the case admit, be positive, made in ample time and with due regard to the observance of good seamanship.

> The Rules of this part mean Part B (Steering and Sailing Rules, 5–19).
> 'If the circumstances of the case admit.' This phrase crops up in many rules from now on and means that this action or direction shall be complied with as long as there are no other factors to make it unsafe to do so. In this case, a positive manoeuvre is requested, but this may not be achievable in a head-on situation in

a narrow channel. However, a safe passing distance could still be achieved by a slight alteration early on, and it would be imperative that the manoeuvre was made with due regard to the observance of good seamanship.

When reading the rules, sometimes reading the words 'if the circumstances of the case admit' throws you off the meaning of the rule. Another way of defining this phrase is by replacing it with 'if possible'. Therefore, these are the actions that should be complied with, unless there is another contributing factor, such as shallow water to one side or other vessels restricting your actions, etc. This is when your judgement and seamanship is required to best interpret the rule.

If it all goes wrong and you end up in court, you will have to prove your good seamanship, against the other party's interpretation of the term.

The Rule also states: 'Any actions you take to avoid a collision should be made in accordance with the rules in this Part;' i.e. Part B: ALL the Steering and Sailing Rules, Sections I, II & III.

Whatever your action, it will always be positive, made in ample time and with due regard to the observance of good seamanship.

(b) Any alteration of course and/or speed to avoid collision shall, if the circumstances of the case admit, be large enough to be readily apparent to another vessel observing visually or by radar; a succession of small alterations of course and/or speed should be avoided.

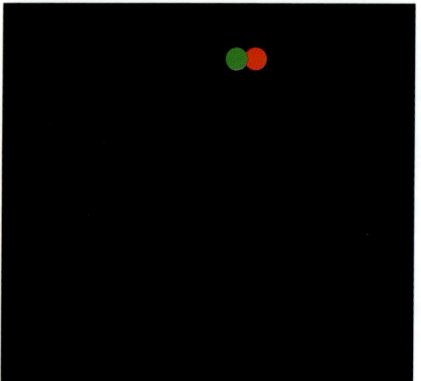
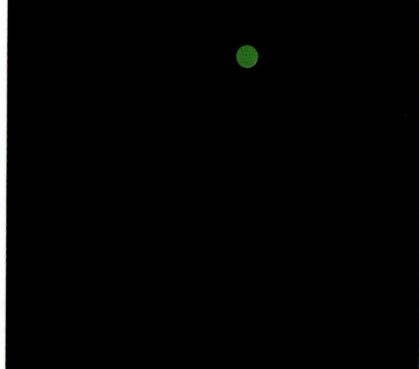

▲ Rule 8(b). How much you alter course is always based on making it clear to the other vessel

'Readily apparent to the other vessel' could mean that at night the other vessel would see an appreciable change in lights or aspect. Therefore, a course change would normally be something near 90 degrees in a crossing situation. The

PART B – STEERING AND SAILING RULES

alteration needs to be readily apparent to the other vessel.

'Readily apparent' by radar gives us another problem as it normally takes longer to establish another vessel's intentions using radar observations. Even when using ARPA or MARPA it takes a few minutes to get a good 'lock' on the other vessel. Therefore, it is important not to act on scanty information.

(c) If there is sufficient sea-room, alteration of course alone may be the most effective action to avoid a close-quarters situation provided that it is made in good time, is substantial and does not result in another close-quarters situation.

Alteration of course is often the most effective and apparent action because it changes the vessel's aspect most quickly. Situations when a speed change can be effective are when approaching vessels are near abeam.

(d) Action taken to avoid collision with another vessel shall be such as to result in passing at a safe distance. The effectiveness of the action shall be carefully checked until the other vessel is finally past and clear.

This is the result, if the above actions listed in Rule 8(a), (b) and (c) have been taken effectively. Compliance with this rule will nearly always be centred on the give-way vessel to 'take early and substantial action to keep well clear', because it is the give-way vessel that has the most responsibility to take action to avoid a collision. If the give-way vessel does not get out of the way, the stand-on vessel may need to take action 'by her manoeuvre alone' (Rule 17(a)(ii)) well in advance of this situation or ultimately 'take such action as will best aid to avoid collision'. Therefore 'passing at a safe distance' is the give-way vessel's main obligation.

'Carefully checked' – any way that we would establish that a risk of collision exists should also be used to 'carefully check' whether 'the other vessel is finally passed and clear'. Methods include:

1. Compass bearings
2. Radar plotting or systematic observation
3. Listening for sounds, etc.

There is no definition of a safe distance and much will depend on 'the circumstances of the case'; for instance, a safe distance when passing behind a vessel will probably be smaller than a safe distance when passing ahead. A safe distance overtaking might be smaller than for a vessel crossing.

(e) If necessary to avoid collision or allow more time to assess the situation, a vessel shall slacken her speed or take all way off by stopping or reversing her means of propulsion.

This rule supports the all-important issue of situation awareness and buying time. 'A vessel' means any vessel: sail, fishing, RAM, power-driven vessel, etc.

The main way of gaining more time and regaining situational awareness in a situation is to slow down. Consider that a vessel travelling at 10 knots will travel one mile in six minutes and at 20 knots two miles in six minutes. If a vessel is spotted at a radar range of six miles and the combined closing speed of your and the other vessel is 30 knots, they will meet in 12 minutes. It is very important to keep watching what is going on and to take early and positive action when required.

This rule will be used in conjunction with Rule 6 as to whether your vessel was going too fast in the conditions; can she 'take proper and effective action to avoid collision and be stopped within a distance appropriate to the prevailing circumstances and conditions'?

(f)
   (i) A vessel which, by any of these Rules, is required not to impede the passage or safe passage of another vessel shall, when required by the circumstances of the case, take early action to allow sufficient sea-room for the safe passage of the other vessel.

The word 'impede' crops up mainly in Rules 9(b), (c) and (d): Narrow Channels; and Rule 10(j) and (l): Traffic Separation Schemes. It also crops up in Rule 18(d)(i), (e) and (f)(i): Responsibilities. In Rules 9 and 10, there are three main vessel types that this applies to, and these are sailing vessels, vessels under 20m and vessels engaged in fishing (although there are others).

The word impede puts a responsibility and obligation only onto the vessel that 'shall not impede'. It does change the final obligation under the rules of the vessel 'not to be impeded'.

Rule 8(f)(i) requires that a vessel shall not impede the passage or safe passage of another vessel that shall not be impeded – therefore a sailing vessel shall not impede a supertanker in a narrow channel. As soon as the sailing vessel establishes that the supertanker is there, she shall 'take early action to allow sufficient sea-room' for her safe passage and not get in her way.

PART B – STEERING AND SAILING RULES

(ii) A vessel required not to impede the passage or safe passage of another vessel is not relieved of this obligation if approaching the other vessel so as to involve risk of collision and shall, when taking action, have full regard to the action which may be required by the Rules of this Part.

> When the impeding rule comes in, it applies when there is no risk of collision (see Rule 8(f)(i)) and also if there is a risk of collision (see Rule 8(f)(ii)). Normally the rules only apply when there is a risk of collision – so Rule 8(f)(ii) overrides the normal ColRegs by keeping the obligation on those vessels that shall not impede, to also 'take early action to allow sufficient searoom' when there is 'a risk of collision'. Therefore, a sailing vessel should not impede a tanker in a narrow channel, whereas in open water the tanker (power) would need to give way to the sailing vessel because of priorities of vessel in Rule 18(a). Realistically our hypothetical tankers obligations actually remain unchanged as Rule 8(f)(iii) states.

(iii) A vessel the passage of which is not to be impeded remains fully obliged to comply with the Rules of this Part when the two vessels are approaching one another so as to involve risk of collision.

> This part of the rule applies to the vessel that shall not be impeded – so let's say the larger vessel is within the narrow channel or following the traffic lane. This states that the 'rules of this part' (Part B – Steering and Sailing Rules – Sections I, II and III) apply to the vessel that should not be impeded.
>
> For instance, the vessel not to be impeded (tanker following a traffic lane in a TSS) would expect that a sailing vessel would take early action to allow sufficient searoom. If the sailing vessel carries on and *does* impede the tanker, the tanker would need to give way because the sailing vessel has a higher priority (Rule 18) and the tanker would need to apply the 'rules of this part'.
>
> It is important to remember that the impeding rule only affects the responsibilities of the vessels that 'shall not impede' and does not affect the responsibility of the vessel 'not to be impeded'.

Rule 9

Narrow channels

> This rule applies not only to narrow channels but also to fairways.

COLLISION REGULATIONS HANDBOOK

◀ Rule 9. Sometimes the byelaws or a chart note defines a narrow channel or fairway

> **MODIFICATIONS TO AND AMPLIFICATIONS OF CERTAIN RULES IN THE DOCKYARD PORT OF PLYMOUTH ORDER 1999.**
> <u>Narrow Channels (Dockyard Port of Plymouth Order 1999, Schedule 2 Rule 2)</u>: The whole of Cattewater comprises a 'Narrow Channel' for the purposes of Rule 9 of the International Regulations for Preventing Collisions at Sea 1972. This means that all vessels under 20 metres in length...

(a) A vessel proceeding along the course of a narrow channel or fairway shall keep as near to the outer limit of the channel or fairway which lies on her starboard side as is safe and practicable.

> NP100 describes a fairway as 'the main navigable channel in the approaches to, or within a river or harbour. Sometimes called a Ship Channel'.
>
> Occasionally a chart, sailing directions or local byelaws will indicate specific narrow channels or fairways, but even if they're not specified, a mariner would use their discretion if it is apparent that the vessel is in an approach channel to or from the sea, or in a buoyed channel.
>
> So we stay on the starboard side of the channel when proceeding. How far we stay to starboard will be as far 'as practicable', depending on depth and hazards, etc. Some channel marks may be in shallow water that would make you run aground if you ran close by them – so you run as close as practicable, taking into account your under-keel clearance.
>
> In restricted visibility, radar could also be used to establish the starboard side of the channel, maybe by parallel indexing or a VRM.

(b) A vessel of less than 20m in length or a sailing vessel shall not impede the passage of a vessel which can safely navigate only within a narrow channel or fairway.

> Small vessels under 20m and all sailing vessels shall not impede the passage of a vessel that can safely only navigate within a narrow channel or fairway; therefore,

PART B – STEERING AND SAILING RULES

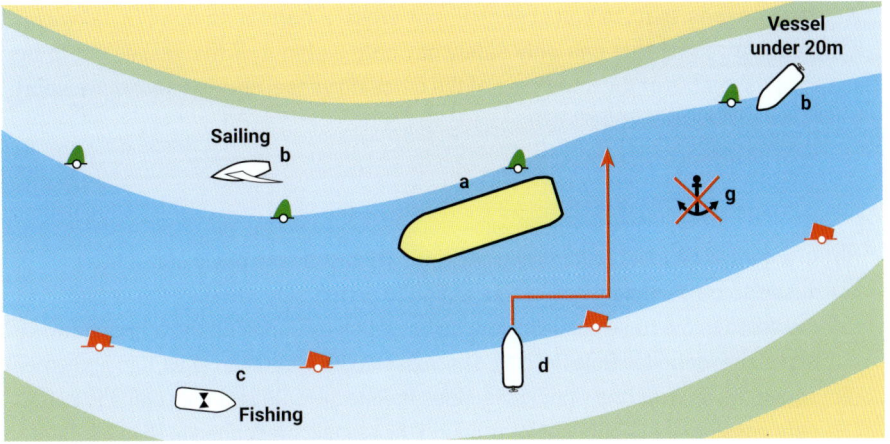

▲ Rule 9. Covers narrow channels but also fairways which might be less well defined

they must take early action to 'allow sufficient searoom for the passage of the other vessel' (Rule 8(f)(i)).

Even if those vessels are unsure if they are impeding, they should assume they are and keep clear.

However, they only need to not impede vessels 'which can safely navigate only within a narrow channel or fairway'. There could be a large vessel that can safely navigate outside the channel and the sail/small vessel obligation is reduced, but how they would then go on to prove it, if there was a collision, is another matter.

(c) A vessel engaged in fishing shall not impede the passage of any other vessel navigating within a narrow channel or fairway.

The key change here is that a fishing vessel shall not impede the passage of ANY OTHER VESSEL navigating within a narrow channel or fairway, whereas sail and vessels under 20m shall not impede the passage of a vessel that can *'only safely navigate in the channel'*.

However, a fishing vessel can fish within a narrow channel or fairway as long as she is not impeding and clears out of the way if and when she needs to.

(d) A vessel shall not cross a narrow channel or fairway if such crossing impedes the passage of a vessel which can safely navigate only within such channel or fairway. The latter vessel may use the sound signal prescribed in Rule 34(d) if in doubt as to the intention of the crossing vessel.

35

'A vessel' means that ANY vessel shall not cross a narrow channel or fairway if it impedes a vessel that can only safely navigate within it. If the vessel 'not to be impeded' is unsure of the intentions of the crossing vessel she can sound five short blasts, as specified in Rule 34(d).

(e)
  (i) In a narrow channel or fairway when overtaking can take place only if the vessel to be overtaken has to take action to permit safe passing, the vessel intending to overtake shall indicate her intention by sounding the appropriate signal prescribed in Rule 34(c)(i). The vessel to be overtaken shall, if in agreement, sound the appropriate signal prescribed in Rule 34(c)(ii) and take steps to permit safe passing. If in doubt she may sound the signals prescribed in Rule 34(d).

If the vessel being overtaken in a narrow channel has to take action to allow safe passing, such as she needs to move over to one side, then the vessel intending to overtake should sound the following sound signals, as listed in Rule 34(c)(i):
- I intend to overtake you on your starboard side: two long and one short.
- I intend to overtake you on your port side: two long and two short. And the vessel being overtaken would sound, according to Rule 34(c)(ii):
- I indicate my agreement: long, short, long, short. And then that vessel would move to one side to allow safe passing. It should be remembered that these signals would only be given when in sight of one another AND NOT IN RESTRICTED VISIBILITY.
- If the vessel being overtaken were in any doubt, she would sound Rule 34(d): five short and rapid blasts.

  (ii) This Rule does not relieve the overtaking vessel of her obligation under Rule 13.

The key obligation under Rule 13 is that 'any vessel overtaking any other vessel shall keep out of the way of the vessel being overtaken'.

(f) A vessel nearing a bend or an area of a narrow channel or fairway where other vessels may be obscured by an intervening obstruction shall navigate with particular alertness and caution and shall sound the appropriate signal prescribed in Rule 34(e).

The sound signal in Rule 34(e) is one long blast. 34(e) also goes on to say that the

PART B – STEERING AND SAILING RULES

◀ Rule 9(f). Vessels obscured in a narrow channel shall sound one prolonged blast

vessel being obscured (which is around the bend) would also answer using one long blast.

Note: This sound signal of one long blast for vessels obscured by a bend can be used in restricted visibility and in normal visibility as there is no indication as to the state of visibility in Rule 34(e).

(g) Any vessel shall, if the circumstances of the case admit, avoid anchoring in a narrow channel.

If for any reason it is imperative to anchor in a narrow channel or fairway (for instance in the event of engine failure), then you would anchor close to one side if possible. It would also be good seamanship to inform the port or controller of the fairway.

Rule 10

Traffic separation schemes

(a) This Rule applies to traffic separation schemes adopted by the Organization and does not relieve any vessel of her obligation under any other Rule.

'Organization' means the IMO.

A list of the IMO-adopted traffic separation schemes (TSS) are listed in the IMO publication *Ships' Routeing*.

COLLISION REGULATIONS HANDBOOK

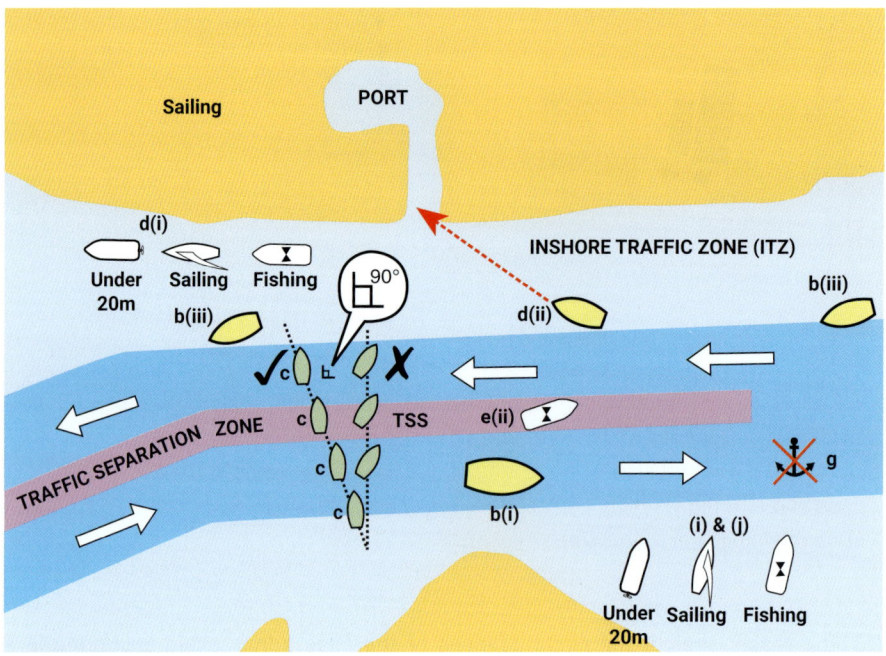

▲ Rule 10

This rule applies to TSS 'adopted' so any rules stated in Rule 10 (including: those vessels that should not impede other vessels; how you manage your vessel when within the TSS; how you enter, exit and cross) only apply to bona-fide TSS and not just shipping lanes.

The term 'does not relieve any vessel of her obligation under any other rule' means that all the standard ColRegs apply to all vessels while in a TSS. Navigating within a TSS confers NO privileges upon anyone.

IMO define the parts of a TSS as:
- 'Traffic Separation Scheme: A routeing measure aimed at the separation of opposing streams of traffic by appropriate means and by the establishment of traffic lanes.
- Traffic lanes: An area within defined limits in which one-way traffic is established. Natural obstacles, including those forming separation zones, may constitute a boundary.
- Separation lines or separation zones:
A zone or line separating the traffic lanes in which ships are proceeding in opposite or nearly opposite directions; or separating a traffic lane from the

PART B – STEERING AND SAILING RULES

adjacent sea area; or separating traffic lanes designated for particular classes of ship proceeding in the same direction.
- Inshore traffic zones: A routeing measure comprising a designated area between the landward boundary of a traffic separation scheme and the adjacent coast to be used in accordance with the provisions of Rule 10(d), as amended, of the International Regulations for Preventing Collisions at Sea, 1972 (COLREGS).

(b) A vessel using a traffic separation scheme shall:
 (i) proceed in the appropriate traffic lane in the general direction of traffic flow for that lane;

Follow the arrows marked on the chart within the TSS – not necessarily parallel to them, but in the same 'general direction'.

 (ii) so far as practicable keep clear of a traffic separation line or separation zone;

Stay away from the outer and inner areas marked in magenta. This stops ambiguity and saves the vessel getting caught up with vessels who are crossing or proceeding in the opposite lane.

 (iii) normally join or leave a traffic lane at the termination of the lane, but when joining or leaving from either side shall do so at as small an angle to the general direction of traffic flow as practicable.

It might be necessary to join or leave along a lane because of the port you are required to visit. Similar to a motorway, these are lanes going in one direction so you join on a slip lane at a shallow angle or join at the start.

(c) A vessel shall, so far as practicable, avoid crossing traffic lanes but if obliged to do so shall cross on a heading as nearly as practicable at right angles to the general direction of traffic flow.

Crossing lanes is unavoidable in many instances, but if a craft can go around a TSS she should. If, however, it is not practicable, then she may cross – think of the

COLLISION REGULATIONS HANDBOOK

> Dover Strait and cross-Channel ferries. In use, when crossing, the vessel's aspect should be at right angles to the vessels in the traffic lane so it is a straightforward crossing situation. This does not mean that her course over ground is at right angles but that her heading is at right angles.

(d)
  (i) A vessel shall not use an inshore traffic zone when she can safely use the appropriate traffic lane within the adjacent traffic separation scheme. However, vessels of less than 20m in length, sailing vessels and vessels engaged in fishing may use the inshore traffic zone.

> Most vessels will be required to use a traffic lane, even a 21m pleasure motorboat or workboat. There are times that a 21m boat may want to stay closer to the shelter of land and therefore requests the controller of the TSS for permission to use the inshore traffic zone (ITZ) rather than the lane.
>
> The term 'may use' means that while sailing, vessels engaged in fishing and under 20m vessels may use an ITZ, they can also use the traffic lane.

  (ii) Notwithstanding sub-paragraph (d)(i), a vessel may use an inshore traffic zone when en route to or from a port, offshore installation or structure, pilot station or any other place situated within the inshore traffic zone, or to avoid immediate danger.

> This is mainly self-explanatory. To avoid 'immediate danger' may be to avoid collision, therefore a vessel may stray into the ITZ to avoid a collision but would then rejoin the traffic lane at a shallow angle.

(e) A vessel other than a crossing vessel or a vessel joining or leaving a lane shall not normally enter a separation zone or cross a separation line except:
  (i) in cases of emergency to avoid immediate danger;

> An emergency could be a loss of propulsion or to avoid another vessel. Hopefully standard collision avoidance should be thought ahead so that neither vessel needs to cross into the separation line or enter the separation zone.

  (ii) to engage in fishing within a separation zone.

PART B – STEERING AND SAILING RULES

> It is possible to fish in a separation zone. Guidance to fishermen is that if they were trawling an area of the zone, they should do so in the same general direction as the traffic lane that they are near to so as not to give the wrong message to vessels proceeding in that lane.
>
> It is also possible to fish in a traffic lane so long as the fishing vessel does not impede the passage of a vessel following the lane.

(f) A vessel navigating in areas near the terminations of traffic separation schemes shall do so with particular caution.

> The entrances and terminations of a TSS are funnels, therefore traffic density and potential conflicts will increase. As traffic density increases, this should prompt a reappraisal of Rule 6, safe speed.

(g) A vessel shall so far as practicable avoid anchoring in a traffic separation scheme or in areas near its terminations.

> The key words here being 'so far as practicable'. Common sense dictates that anchoring in a traffic lane would be like stopping in the centre lane of a motorway. However, occasionally needs must if the vessel were adrift and might drift through the oncoming traffic.

(h) A vessel not using a traffic separation scheme shall avoid it by as wide a margin as is practicable.

(i) A vessel engaged in fishing shall not impede the passage of any vessel following a traffic lane.

> Once again, a fishing vessel shall not impede the passage of *any vessel* following the lane, whereas the vessel under 20m or sailing vessel shall not impede the safe passage of a 'power-driven vessel' following the lane.

(j) A vessel of less than 20m in length or a sailing vessel shall not impede the safe passage of a power-driven vessel following a traffic lane.

> Rule 8(f)(i), (ii) and (iii) give details on how not to impede. This would generally

apply to vessels crossing the TSS. However, *any* vessel can use a traffic lane, but if a small vessel or a sailing vessel were using the lane, they should still not impede the safe passage of a power-driven vessel following the lane.

'Not impede the *safe passage*', occurs in a TSS Rule 10(i,j) and applies to sailing and vessels under 20m; and Rule 18(d): CBD. In these circumstances, the vessel not to be impeded might have room to alter course, for instance a traffic lane could be a few miles wide, allowing the vessel following the lane to alter and pass clear of the vessel that should not impede (eg sailing vessel). However, there may be times that either due to a narrow lane, or other traffic restricting the vessels actions or navigational hazards, the vessel not to be impeded cannot manoeuvre and the obligation falls back onto the other vessel not to impede. Use of five short blasts would only be given if the vessel not to be impeded cannot alter because of its circumstance and if required by Rule 34(d).

(k) A vessel restricted in her ability to manoeuvre when engaged in an operation for the maintenance of safety of navigation in a traffic separation scheme is exempted from complying with this Rule to the extent necessary to carry out the operation.

An example of this would be a vessel showing the lights and shapes of a RAM working on a navigational mark in or adjacent to the TSS. When this vessel has finished their work in the TSS, she would no longer be exempt and would have to conform to the rules of this part.

(l) A vessel restricted in her ability to manoeuvre when engaged in an operation for the laying, servicing or picking up of a submarine cable, within a traffic separation scheme, is exempted from complying with this Rule to the extent necessary to carry out the operation.

A cable could be lying diagonally across the traffic lane or TSS, running to/from an offshore installation or island. Obviously if a vessel was laying or servicing this cable it would not be able to 'proceed in the general direction of the lane or cross at right angles to the lane'.

Note: When considering traffic lanes, quite often it is possible for a vessel to manoeuvre within a traffic lane and give way to another vessel without the requirement for stepping outside of a lane. Lanes are normally quite wide (2–4 miles), although this is sometimes not the case.

SECTION II – Conduct of vessels in sight of one another

Rule 11

Application

Rules in this Section apply to vessels in sight of one another.

> Rules 11–18 apply when you are in sight of the other vessel. The definition of 'in sight' is given in Rule 3(k): 'Vessels shall be deemed to **be in sight of one another** only when one can be observed visually from the other.' By default, Rules 11–18 would not be applied in Restricted Visibility (Rule 19), that is until the other vessel looms out of the fog and is then 'in sight'.

Rule 12

Sailing vessels

> For sailboats when racing, there are also the 'Racing Rules of Sailing' (RRS) that are written and administered by World Sailing, an international organization concerning sailing and sail racing. The RRS deal with large groups of sailing boats when racing and rounding a racing mark or en route to a mark (turning point).
>
> When sailing vessels involved in racing meet any vessel that is not racing, then the IMO ColRegs take precedent. Therefore, a hail from a racing sailboat of 'give way because we are racing' to a sailing vessel that is not racing does not hold any power.

COLLISION REGULATIONS HANDBOOK

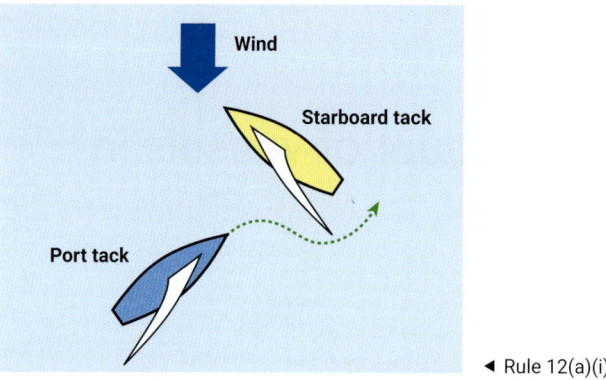

◀ Rule 12(a)(i)

(a) When two sailing vessels are approaching one another, so as to involve risk of collision, one of them shall keep out of the way of the other as follows:
  (i) when each has the wind on a different side, the vessel which has the wind on the port side shall keep out of the way of the other;

> Sailing boats are said to be on starboard or port 'tack'. Those that are on port tack shall keep out of the way of those on starboard tack. The tack is determined by which way the wind is coming over the boat and, therefore, where the main sail is positioned. Wind coming over the starboard side/mainsail to port = starboard tack..

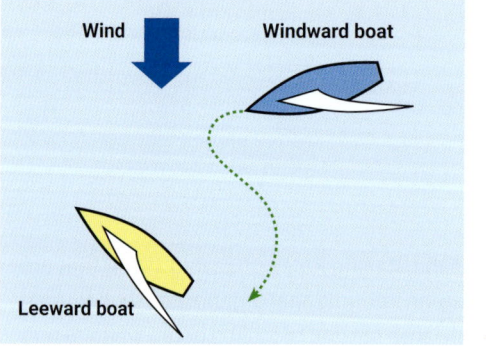

◀ Rule 12(a)(ii)

  (ii) when both have the wind on the same side, the vessel which is to windward shall keep out of the way of the vessel which is to leeward;
  (iii) if a vessel with the wind on the port side sees a vessel to windward and cannot determine with certainty whether the other vessel has the wind on the port or on the starboard side, she shall keep out of the way of the other.

PART B – STEERING AND SAILING RULES

◀ Rule 12(a)(iii)

This rule puts the onus on the port tack boat when, if she cannot establish the tack of the other vessel upwind, then she should give way. Times when this may happen could be: when looking at a vessel that is in the sun; if the boat has a spinnaker hoisted, or if both main and foresail are carried on different sides and it is difficult to tell the difference.

◀ Rule 12(b). Windward side in this instance would be the starboard side 'opposite to that which the largest fore-and-aft sail is carried'

COLLISION REGULATIONS HANDBOOK

(b) For the purposes of this Rule the windward side shall be deemed to be the side opposite to that on which the mainsail is carried or, in the case of a square-rigged vessel, the side opposite to that on which the largest fore-and-aft sail is carried.

To ensure there is no ambiguity, this makes it clear that the windward side is the side opposite the mainsail.

Rule 13

Overtaking

(a) Notwithstanding anything contained in the Rules of Part B, Sections I and II, any vessel overtaking any other shall keep out of the way of the vessel being overtaken.

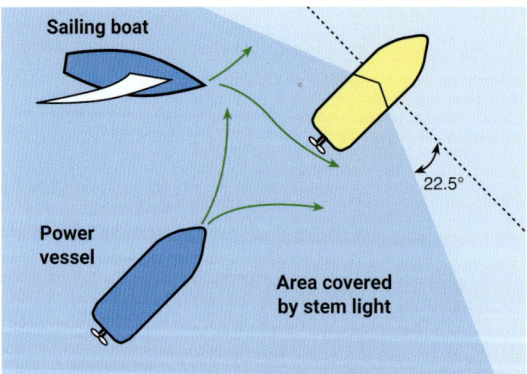

◀ Rule 13(a). Any vessel overtaking any other shall keep out of the way

To decipher this first sentence:
- Part B = Steering and sailing rules
- Section I = In all states of visibility
- Section II = In sight of one another

The rest of this rule overrides ALL others. For instance, Rule 18 (Responsibilities) would normally mean that a power-driven vessel would keep clear of a sailing vessel, but Rule 13 states: 'ANY vessel overtaking ANY other shall keep out of the

PART B – STEERING AND SAILING RULES

way of the vessel being overtaken.' Therefore, even a tug and tow, RAM or sailing vessel when overtaking a straightforward power-driven vessel shall keep clear of the vessel being overtaken.

In most of the other rules, it states that a risk of collision shall exist before an action is taken. However, when overtaking, if you are overtaking another vessel, you shall keep clear whatever the circumstance.

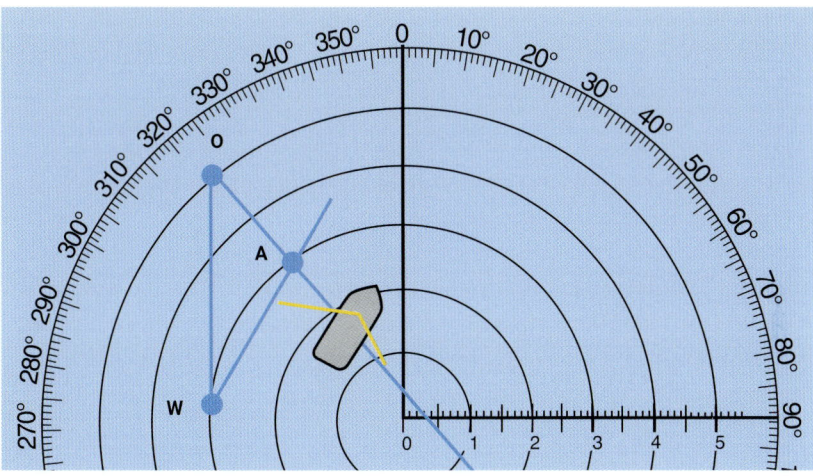

▲ Rule 13(b). A radar contact may need to be interrogated to establish its actual aspect (WA) and not its relative direction (OA)

(b) A vessel shall be deemed to be overtaking when coming up with another vessel from a direction more than 22.5 degrees abaft her beam, that is, in such a position with reference to the vessel she is overtaking, that at night she would be able to see only the sternlight of that vessel but neither of her sidelights.

The aspect of the sternlight at night is given in Rule 21(c).

'Sternlight' means a white light placed as nearly as practicable at the stern showing an unbroken light over an arc of the horizon of 135 degrees and so fixed as to show the light 67.5 degrees from astern on each side of the vessel.

The rule states 'more than 22.5 degrees abaft the beam', suggesting that 'at' 22.5 degrees abaft the beam it may be a crossing situation. However, Rule 13(c) states that if a vessel is in any doubt, she shall assume she is.

Whether we are at the point of overtaking is sometimes difficult to establish when using radar. There may be a contact that looks like it is a crossing vessel (OA), but after working out her heading (WA) rather than her relative aspect, we may be overtaking her. For example, the first and last contact OA at first glance looks like the vessel is a crossing vessel and as such we would be stand-on. However, after systematically plotting the contact, and calculating the aspect, it is established we are in the overtaking zone and therefore need to 'keep out of the way' of the other vessel.

Annex 1, Positioning and technical details of lights and shapes, Section 9 Horizontal Sectors, discusses the cut-out of sternlights and the emergence of masthead and side lights. There are possibilities where the lights may be seen either together or reduce in their intensity at the outer edges of their sector, which might allow doubt to creep in between approximately 110–115 degrees for those observing the lights.

(c) When a vessel is in any doubt as to whether she is overtaking another, she shall assume that this is the case and act accordingly.

There are not many times within the ColRegs that we are told to 'assume'. However, this is one of them, so for example if we are closing a vessel at night and we are getting her sternlight and sidelight alternately, we are then 'in doubt' as to whether we are overtaking. If we have a doubt, then we should assume we are overtaking.

(d) Any subsequent alteration of the bearing between the two vessels shall not make the overtaking vessel a crossing vessel within the meaning of these Rules or relieve her of the duty of keeping clear of the overtaken vessel until she is finally past and clear.

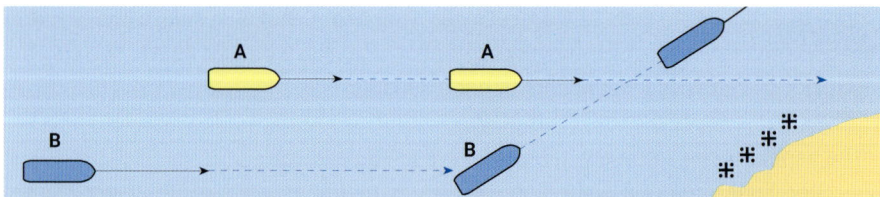

▲ Rule 13(d)

The Rule applies even if an appreciable bearing change is evident. If a vessel (B) is coming up relatively close to another (A) from more than 22.5 degrees abaft her starboard beam, draws ahead, and then subsequently turns to port to come on to a crossing course, she IS NOT RELIEVED of the duty of keeping clear and she is not deemed a crossing vessel.

We are an overtaking vessel until we are finally past and clear.

PART B – STEERING AND SAILING RULES

Rule 14

Head-on situation

(a) When two power-driven vessels are meeting on reciprocal or nearly reciprocal courses so as to involve risk of collision each shall alter her course to starboard so that each shall pass on the port side of the other.

> 'Each shall alter' makes this rule quite special as both vessels have an obligation to take action. The term power-driven vessel will not mean sailing vessels, RAM, fishing, etc. as other issues may dictate what they do, such as the wind direction for sail boats, whether they have gear out, or whether there is a priority of vessels that requires only one vessel to act.

(b) Such a situation shall be deemed to exist when a vessel sees the other ahead or nearly ahead and by night she would see the masthead lights of the other in a line or nearly in a line and or both sidelights and by day she observes the corresponding aspect of the other vessel.

> There is a little bit of vagueness built in here because if she sees a vessel ahead or nearly ahead by looking at the masthead and sidelights there is always a possibility with the sidelights that there is a fade-out in the last 1–3 degrees. However, Rule 14(c) clears up any ambiguity.
> The rule also applies to the ship's head and not the course over ground of the vessel.

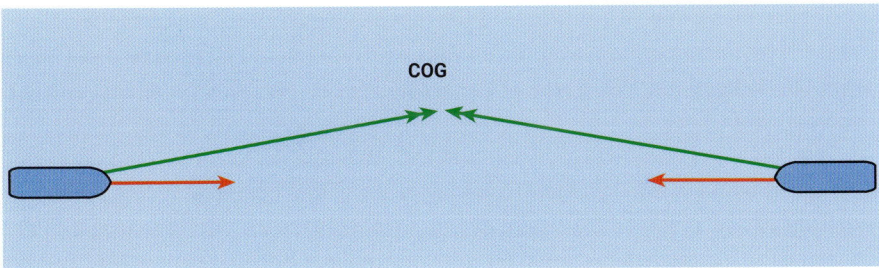

▲ Rule 14(b)

COLLISION REGULATIONS HANDBOOK

(c) When a vessel is in any doubt as to whether such a situation exists, she shall assume that it does exist and act accordingly.

One of the few times we 'assume' within the ColRegs. So, if we are unsure as to whether we are head-on, we probably are.

Rule 15

Crossing situation

When two power-driven vessels are crossing so as to involve risk of collision, the vessel which has the other on her own starboard side shall keep out of the way and shall, if the circumstances of the case admit, avoid crossing ahead of the other vessel.

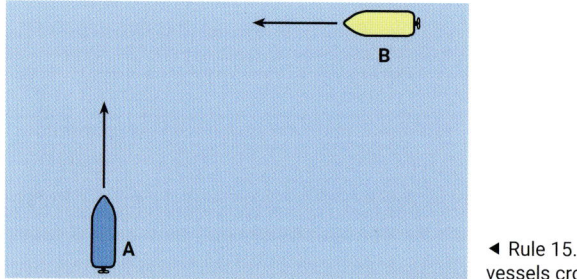

◀ Rule 15. Concerns two power-driven vessels crossing

Once again this applies to two power-driven vessels only. Two sailing boats have their own rules (Rule 12), and Rule 18 (Responsibilities) takes care of all the other vessels; for instance, if a power-driven vessel (PDV) and a sailing vessel meet, the PDV has to keep out of the way of the sailing vessel, from whichever side she is approaching.

The requirement to 'avoid crossing ahead' only applies to a PDV and another PDV. In other rules, such as Rule 18, it may be the safest course of action to cross well ahead of a vessel with gear out astern, so long as the distance ahead is a safe one and the manoeuvre is carried out with due regard to good seamanship.

It should also be remembered that a tug and tow are classed as a PDV, unless the tug is displaying lights or shapes for RAM. Therefore, a standard tug and tow

PART B – STEERING AND SAILING RULES

> not showing ball-diamond-ball or lights to suit would be classed as a PDV and, therefore, you would avoid passing ahead if you were also a PDV.
>
> A vessel underway but not making way (lying stopped) is still subject to the ColRegs. Therefore, it should still take action for vessels coming from her starboard side or ahead. A vessel lying underway but not making way also needs to keep a good look-out and take action as per normal ColRegs.
>
> This rule is modified slightly when particular vessels are crossing in certain situations: narrow channels, fairways (Rule 9(b), (c), (d)) and traffic lanes (Rule 10(i), (j)). In these situations, the vessel in the narrow channel, fairway or traffic lane will still apply the crossing situation rules and be either stand-on or give-way. However, on occasion, some vessels identified in Rules 9 and 10 (sailing vessels, under 20m and vessels engaged in fishing) have an obligation not to impede a vessel that can only safely navigate within the narrow channel or travelling in the traffic lane. The obligation of the vessel not to be impeded in the narrow channel or lane remains unchanged – if the vessel required not to impede does impede and the vessel not to be impeded is normally the give-way vessel – it remains the give-way vessel (Rule 8(f)(i), (ii), (iii)).
>
> There is a fundamental difference when a power-driven vessel is in a crossing situation with a CBD. This is because a CBD is still deemed a 'power-driven vessel', as per the definition in Rule 3(h). Therefore, the give-way obligation of the CBD in a crossing situation for a power-driven vessel on her starboard side remains unchanged.
>
> However, a PDV, sailing vessel or fishing vessel has an obligation to not impede a vessel that is displaying the lights or shapes of a CBD as stated in Rule 18(d), but if those vessels do impede, the responsibility could still fall to the CBD to keep clear because at the end of the day it is still a PDV.

Rule 16

Action by give-way vessel

Every vessel which is directed to keep out of the way of another vessel shall, so far as possible, take early and substantial action to keep well clear.

> The words 'every vessel' make it clear that this rule applies to all vessels when they are the give-way vessel.
> What do you do if you are the give-way vessel?
> - Take early and substantial action.

> **Why?**
> - To keep well clear.
>
> To take early action you would have:
> - Kept a proper look-out under Rule 5.
> - Established whether a risk of collision exists under Rule 7.
>
> To keep well clear you would have:
> - Been at a safe speed (Rule 6) so that you can take appropriate action.
> - Been able to take action in sufficient time (Rule 8) and therefore had the bridge adequately manned with people who could take control, when required.
>
> This rule does not say what action to take, therefore, all actions and turns to starboard and port are possible, unless another rule or the act of good seamanship says otherwise.

Rule 17

Action by stand-on vessel

(a)

    (i) Where one of two vessels is to keep out of the way the other shall keep her course and speed.

> The stand-on vessel has to keep her course and speed. Otherwise, she would not be making her intentions clear to the other vessel.
>
>   She also needs to keep her course and speed so that the other vessel can make a decision as to whether to turn to port, starboard or slow down.
>
>   The stand-on vessel could be any vessel, PDV, sail, fishing, RAM, CBD or NUC.

    (ii) The latter vessel may however take action to avoid collision by her manoeuvre alone, as soon as it becomes apparent to her that the vessel required to keep out of the way is not taking appropriate action in compliance with these Rules.

> The latter vessel means the stand-on vessel.
>
> 'Manoeuvre alone': this could be a turn or a reduction or increase of speed. It should be noted that any manoeuvre that the 'stand-on' vessel takes should be

PART B – STEERING AND SAILING RULES

such that it does not conflict with the manoeuvre the give-way vessel would probably take if she decides to turn late.

Therefore, turning to port in a crossing situation would be dangerous and possibly slowing might also be problematic if the vessel did eventually turn to starboard and go behind you. Therefore, possibly the safest option would be a turn to starboard as this would at least open the gap up and give more time.

The term 'as soon as it becomes apparent' would be the point at which it becomes apparent that the give-way vessel is not taking action. You would have already sounded five short blasts or given five flashes and waited to see the other vessel's intentions. While standing on with caution, your engines would be ready for manoeuvre and the vessel manually helmed and not on autopilot.

(b) When, from any cause, the vessel required to keep her course and speed finds herself so close that collision cannot be avoided by the action of the give-way vessel alone, she shall take such action as will best aid to avoid collision.

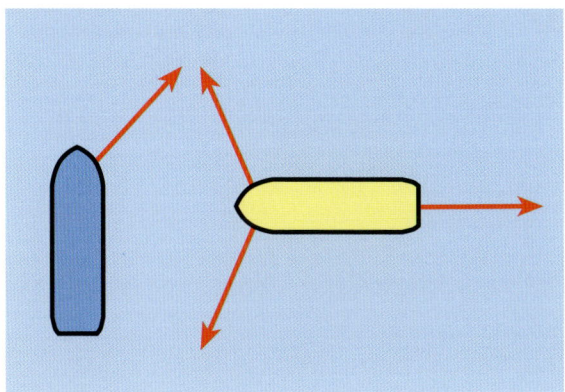

◄ Rule 17(b). When so close that both vessels need to take action, we can take any action that will best avoid collision

Because of the closeness of both vessels in this situation, both vessels would need to take action to avoid a collision. Therefore, if she gets into this position, she can use any manoeuvre to best avoid a collision. So, when it has got to this point when there is a high chance of collision, any action can be taken, if this best avoids a collision. Rule 2(b) also states that we 'may make a departure from these Rules necessary to avoid immediate danger.'

COLLISION REGULATIONS HANDBOOK

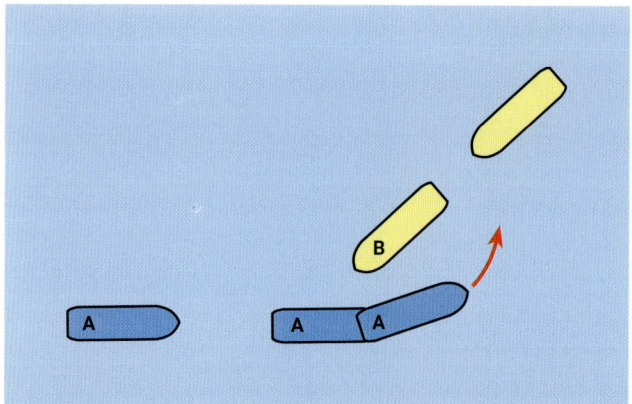

◀ Rule 17(b). 'When so close that collision cannot be avoided by the action of the give way vessel alone, she shall take such action as will best avoid collision'. So while not an easy choice, a turn to port may be the only option as a last resort.

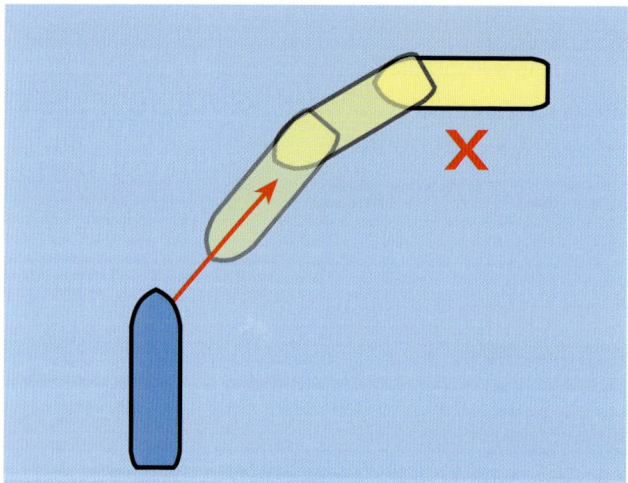

◀ Rule 17(c). If you are a stand-on PDV with another PDV in a crossing situation and have to act because the give-way vessel is failing to act – don't turn to port, just in case the give-way vessel turns late to go behind you

(c) A power-driven vessel which takes action in a crossing situation in accordance with sub-paragraph (a)(ii) of this Rule to avoid collision with another power-driven vessel shall, if the circumstances of the case admit, not alter course to port for a vessel on her own port side.

> This rule only works with 17(a)(ii). Remember this rule is about one PDV and another PDV. It does not apply for a PDV and a sail boat, fishing vessel, RAM, NUC, etc., because a PDV can alter either way for these craft as she is not the 'stand-on' vessel but the give-way vessel.

PART B – STEERING AND SAILING RULES

▼ Rule 17

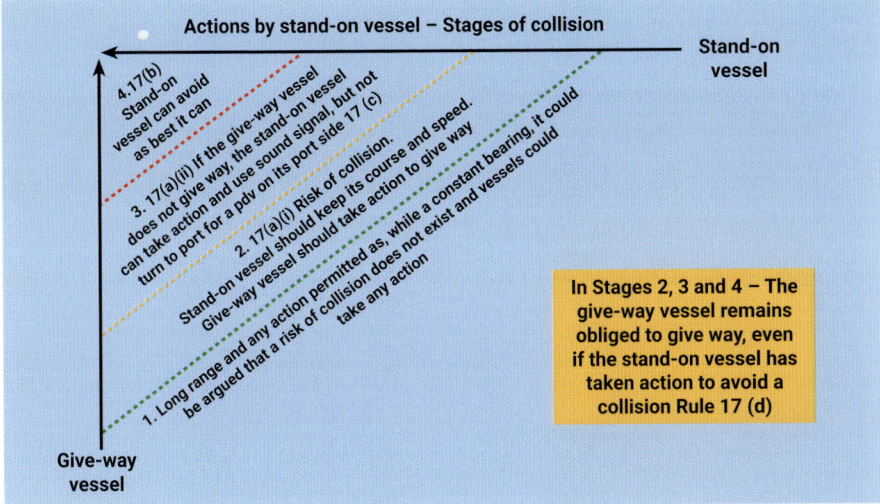

(d) This Rule does not relieve the give-way vessel of her obligation to keep out of the way.

The allowance for the stand-on vessel to get out of the way of the give-way vessel could lead to lots of give-way vessels ignoring the rule and standing on. Rule 17(d) states that this is not the case and the give-way vessel should still fulfil her obligations.

There is, however, a condition that when vessels are far enough apart, while they may be on a constant bearing, they are so far away that it would be unwise to assume that they are actually on a collision course as they may do many things before getting close enough for there to be an issue. Therefore, there are several 'stages' to a collision.

Rule 18

Responsibilities between vessels

Except where Rules 9, 10 and 13 otherwise require:

This exception identifies the special cases when 'higher priority' vessels have to make allowances for 'lower priority' vessels. Rules 9, 10 and 13 stipulate:

COLLISION REGULATIONS HANDBOOK

- Rule 9 requires vessels under 20m, sailing vessels and fishing vessels and crossing vessel not to impede the safe passage of a vessel in a narrow channel or fairway.
- Rule 10 similarly requires vessels under 20m, sailing vessels and fishing vessels not to impede the safe passage of a vessel using a traffic lane.
- Rule 13 states that any vessel overtaking another shall keep clear, therefore a RAM overtaking a PDV shall keep clear of the PDV.

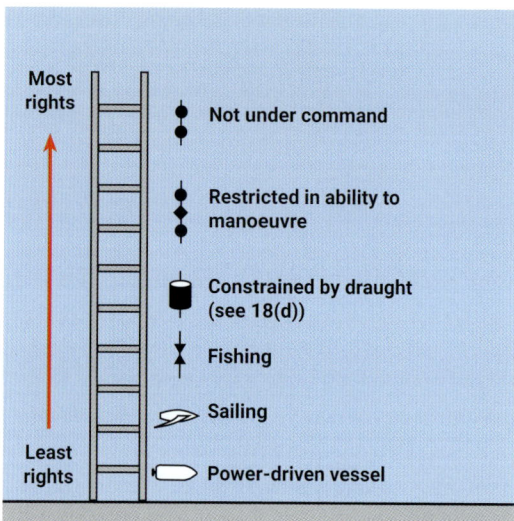

◀ Rule 18. Vessels at the bottom of the ladder, keep out of the way of vessels higher up the ladder. The CBD always remains a PDV, but those vessels below on the ladder are told not to impede its safe passage

(a) A power-driven vessel underway shall keep out of the way of:
  (i) a vessel not under command;
  (ii) a vessel restricted in her ability to manoeuvre;
  (iii) a vessel engaged in fishing;
  (iv) a sailing vessel.
(b) A sailing vessel underway shall keep out of the way of:
  (i) a vessel not under command;
  (ii) a vessel restricted in her ability to manoeuvre;
  (iii) a vessel engaged in fishing.
(c) A vessel engaged in fishing when underway shall, so far as possible, keep out of the way of:
  (i) a vessel not under command;
  (ii) a vessel restricted in her ability to manoeuvre.
(d)
  (i) Any vessel other than a vessel not under command or a vessel restricted in her

PART B – STEERING AND SAILING RULES

ability to manoeuvre shall, if the circumstances of the case admit, avoid impeding the safe passage of a vessel constrained by her draught, exhibiting the signals in Rule 28.

> Constrained by draught and impeding:
>
> There is a noted difference here because in all other cases a certain vessel shall 'keep out of the way of' another type of vessel. Rule 18(d)(i) changes this when it involves 'a vessel constrained by her draught exhibiting three all-round reds or a cylinder' because instead of a PDV, sailing vessel and vessel engaged in fishing 'keeping out of the way of' a vessel CBD, they must now 'avoid impeding' the safe passage of a vessel CBD.
>
> Rules 9 and 10 discuss application of the impeding rules in narrow channels/fairways and traffic separation schemes and this should really cover them all. However, Rule 18(d) also ensures that if a CBD vessel is displaying her signals, wherever she may be, then PDVs, sailing boats and vessels engaged in fishing shall not impede the CBD's safe passage.
>
> The reason for this subtle change is that in Rule 3(h), a CBD vessel is defined as a power-driven vessel, while a RAM and NUC are not (Rule 3(f), (g)). Because of this, a CBD vessel may still end up being a give-way vessel to a PDV, sailing boat or vessel engaged in fishing, if those vessels carry on impeding the CBD's passage.
>
> As a CBD is still deemed a 'power-driven vessel' (Rule 3), in a crossing situation the obligation of the CBD for a vessel on her starboard side remains unchanged. However, the stand-on PDV has an obligation to not impede. When the stand-on PDV takes action to not impede, she would avoid turning to port (Rule 17(c)), so would probably either slow down or turn to starboard and parallel her course until finally past and clear.
>
> As the CBD is technically still a power-driven vessel (Rule 3), it still has an obligation to keep clear of sailing vessels and vessels engaged in fishing (Rule 18(a)) and overall responsibility rests with the CBD Rule (8(f)(iii)). However, Rule 18(d) asks PDVs, sail and fishing vessels to not impede her passage. If a CBD did have to keep out of the way she could only reasonably do that by adjusting her speed.
>
> A vessel constrained by her draught would give way to vessels not under command and restricted in their ability to manoeuvre.

(ii)   A vessel constrained by her draught shall navigate with particular caution having full regard to her special condition.

> Therefore, she should apply Rules 5 and 6 and reduce her speed; she should apply the principles of safe watchkeeping and be on manual steering and have increased look-out. In the event of having to get out of the way of another vessel, she would

COLLISION REGULATIONS HANDBOOK

probably only be able to slow or increase her speed (most probably slow) because of her draught in relation to the available depth and width of navigable water, she is severely restricted in her ability to deviate from the course she is following. Increasing speed would be unlikely as this would also induce more squat effect, reducing the under-keel clearance further.

(e) A seaplane on the water shall, in general, keep well clear of all vessels and avoid impeding their navigation. In circumstances, however, where risk of collision exists, she shall comply with the Rules of this Part.

(f)
- (i) A WIG craft shall, when taking off, landing and in flight near the surface, keep well clear of all other vessels and avoid impeding their navigation;
- (ii) A WIG craft operating on the water surface shall comply with the Rules of this Part as a power-driven vessel.

Generally, seaplanes when on the water or taking off, and WIGs when on the water or taking off/landing shall avoid impeding other vessels' navigation. Therefore, they will allow safe passage to the other vessels, but if they get into a situation where a risk of collision exists, then they will become PDVs and act accordingly.

Impeding vessels

What	Narrow channel or Fairway	TSS	CBD	Other
PDV	X when crossing		X	
PDV under 20m	X	X	X	
Sail	X	X	X	
Fishing	X	X	X	
Any vessel	X when crossing			
RAM	X when crossing			
NUC	X when crossing			
WIG	X by default	X by default	X by default	Keep clear of vessels and avoid impeding their navigation
Seaplane	X by default	X by default	X by default	

SECTION III – Conduct of vessels in restricted visibility

The rules of Part B, Section I, apply together with this rule. Rules in Section II do not apply. It is important to note that when in restricted visibility and not in sight of one another, the rules of sailing vessels, overtaking, head-on, crossing, give-way, stand-on and responsibilities between vessels no longer apply (until a vessel emerges out of the restricted visibility and you can see them again).

The concept of 'give-way' and 'stand-on' vessels does not apply in restricted visibility.

Note: Restricted visibility is not just fog. Rule 3(l) states: 'The term "restricted visibility" means any condition in which visibility is restricted by fog, mist, falling snow, heavy rainstorms, sandstorms or any other similar causes.'

Rule 19

Conduct of vessels in restricted visibility

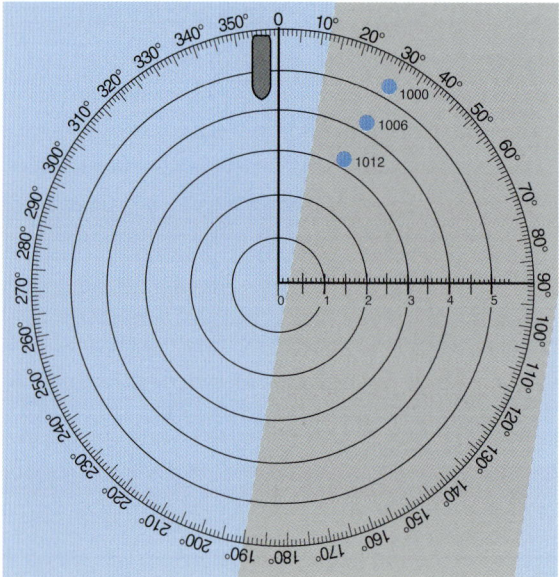

◀ Rule 19(a)

(a) This Rule applies to vessels not in sight of one another when navigating in or near an area of restricted visibility.

This often-misread rule states that for this rule to apply:

1. Vessels must not be in sight of one another.
2. They are operating 'in or near' areas of restricted visibility.

For instance, in the illustration above, the series of three plots observed by radar are in the shaded area representing restricted visibility. Our vessel is positioned in the centre of the circle, and the '0°' line is our heading.

We are not in sight of the series of contacts on our starboard side, therefore this is treated under Section III, Rule 19. The vessel fine on our port bow would be treated under Section II, Rule 14, because even though we are operating in or near areas of restricted visibility, we are in sight of this vessel ahead.

(b) Every vessel shall proceed at a safe speed adapted to the prevailing circumstances and conditions of restricted visibility. A power-driven vessel shall have her engines ready for immediate manoeuvre.

PART B – STEERING AND SAILING RULES

This is a requirement to reassess ALL the factors stipulated in Rule 6 to take into account restricted visibility, and modify your speed accordingly. Usually a vessel shall 'proceed at a safe speed so that she can take proper and effective action to avoid collision and be stopped within a distance appropriate to the prevailing circumstances and conditions'. Additionally, Rule 19(b) ensures that engines are 'ready for immediate manoeuvre'. This may mean that steering is in manual and not in auto mode, the power and engines are manned to allow easy and fast adjustment, especially as we will find that we may need to 'reduce speed to a minimum and take all way off', for example in Rule 19(e).

(c) Every vessel shall have due regard to the prevailing circumstances and conditions of restricted visibility when complying with the Rules of Section I of this Part.

This states that when applying the other relevant rules (Section I: Look-out, Safe speed, Risk of collision, Action to avoid, Narrow channels and TSS) with Rule 19, we should weight those rules with the conditions of restricted visibility. For instance:

Rule 5 'Look-out' would be mainly by hearing and radar as sight is not possible. Look-outs might be increased, especially for vessels without operational radar, and those with radar might have a dedicated radar look-out. Bridge doors may be left open to increase hearing of signals. AIS targets may be interrogated and greater awareness of other vessels' movements would be used by monitoring VHF and VTS, reviewing AIS and radar to build a greater situational awareness of what may be around the vessel.

Rule 6 'Safe speed' will be using a lot of Rule 6(b) 'additionally vessels fitted with operational radar'.

Rule 7 'Risk of collision' increases the use of radar, warns of scanty information, promotes long-range plotting and systematic plotting.

Rule 8 'Actions to avoid' tells us that our actions should be large enough to be readily apparent to vessels observing by radar. In restricted visibility we may wish to increase our CPA limits and magnitude of course or speed alterations to ensure they are, in fact, 'readily apparent'.

In other words, ALL the actions that would normally be required under Section I must now be 'stepped up a gear' once restricted visibility is encountered.

(d) A vessel which detects by radar alone the presence of another vessel shall determine if a close-quarters situation is developing and/or risk of collision exists. If so, she shall take avoiding action in ample time, provided that when such action consists of an alteration of course, so far as possible the following shall be avoided:

(i) an alteration of course to port for a vessel forward of the beam, other than for a vessel being overtaken;

(ii) an alteration of course towards a vessel abeam or abaft the beam.

Key points:

1) Rule 19(d) only applies when a vessel has detected another by 'radar alone'. She has not visually seen or heard it. Rule 19(e) discusses our actions when we 'hear' a vessel.

We might hear a vessel when within two nautical miles of her as per the 'audible range table' of sound signals (Annex III). When we also consider that Rule 7(b) states that to make proper use of radar equipment, we should undertake long-range scanning

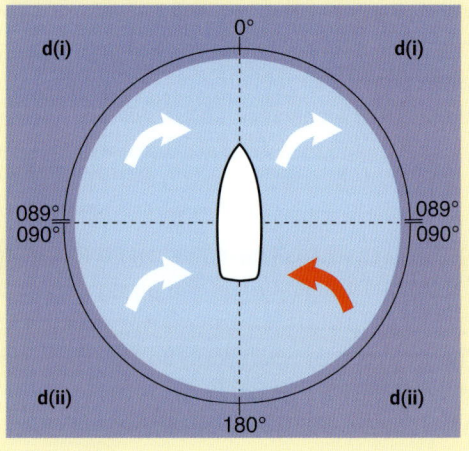

▲ Rule 19(d)

and systematic plotting – we could take from these two points that Rule 19(d) really applies when using radar on a 12- or 6-mile range, but when under two nautical miles and when we can hear another vessel, this rule may not apply with such force.

2) Usually, we are told to determine whether a risk of collision exists (Rule 7(a)). However, now we are determining whether 'a close-quarters situation is developing and/or risk of collision exists'. If these conditions do not exist, we do nothing but continue to carefully monitor the situation.

3) We would expect both vessels to 'take action' and in 'ample time'.

4) Rule 19(d)(i) and (ii) then tell us what not to do:

19(d)(i) means that 'so far as possible' our options are to turn to starboard or slow down for a vessel forward of the beam (so 0–89 degrees either side of the bow), unless you are overtaking a vessel, when it is possible to turn to port.

19(d)(ii) means that 'so far as possible' we should not turn towards a vessel abeam or abaft the beam (so from 90 degrees port side through the stern to 90 degrees starboard side).

So, if the approaching vessel were on our port aft side we would turn to starboard and if she is on our starboard aft side we would turn to port. The approaching vessel would also act accordingly as both vessels have a responsibility to take action.

It would not normally be prudent to slow down for a vessel abaft the beam as it may make the time to closest point of approach (TCPA) shorter.

PART B – STEERING AND SAILING RULES

(e) Except where it has been determined that a risk of collision does not exist, every vessel which hears apparently forward of her beam the fog signal of another vessel, or which cannot avoid a close-quarters situation with another vessel forward of her beam, shall reduce her speed to the minimum at which she can be kept on her course. She shall, if necessary, take all her way off and in any event navigate with extreme caution until danger of collision is over.

> This rule realistically comes in at shorter ranges when a fog signal of another vessel is heard. As the audible range of a fog signal is often two nautical miles or less, the other vessel is going to be close. If for instance the combined approach speeds of the two vessels is 20 knots (10 knots each), the two vessels would meet in six minutes.
>
> The rule starts with the exception of 'except where it has been determined...', so if it has been determined that a risk does not exist, for instance by systematic plotting of a contact on radar, you do not need to do anything except stay vigilant and carefully monitor until the other vessel has passed and is clear. But can you be 100 per cent certain that the fog signal you have heard is that of the vessel you have been plotting?
>
> Therefore, if the fog signal is heard forward of the beam, speed should be reduced. If all way is taken off, remember that your sound signal will change to two long blasts for a power-driven vessel. Once stopped, can you take 'proper and effective action to avoid collision'?
>
> Note: Remember that manoeuvring signals are not used in restricted visibility Rule 34(a).
>
> The rules would be used in the following sequence in restricted visibility:
>
> - Rule 5 Look-out
>   By radar and hearing predominantly – increasing look-out as required.
> - Rule 6 Safe speed
>   Have engines ready for manoeuvre and be able to be stopped. Also use radar and adjust speed accordingly.
> - Rule 7 Risk of collision
>   Use radar on long-range scanning, and hearing. Plot ALL targets detected ARPA/MARPA/VRM/EBL.
> - Rule 19 Restricted visibility
>   Use either the radar (19(d)) or sound (19(e)) rules.
> - Rule 8 Action to avoid
>   Positive, in good time, readily apparent, check until clear, readily apparent to a vessel observing by radar.
>
> Refer to MGN 369 for further details.

PART C – LIGHTS AND SHAPES

Rule 20

Application

(a) Rules in this Part shall be complied with in all weathers.
(b) The Rules concerning lights shall be complied with from sunset to sunrise and during such times no other lights shall be exhibited, except such lights as cannot be mistaken for the lights specified in these Rules or do not impair their visibility or distinctive character, or interfere with the keeping of a proper look-out.

> Sunrise and sunset are defined as when the sun's upper limb (top of the sun) is on the horizon.
> 'Interfere with the keeping of a proper look-out':
> Not only do navigation lights need to come on, but other illumination lights, either on deck or on the bridge, should go off so that a proper look-out can be kept and other vessels have the best chance of identifying our vessel's navigation lights.

(c) The lights prescribed by these Rules shall, if carried, also be exhibited from sunrise to sunset in restricted visibility and may be exhibited in all other circumstances when it is deemed necessary.

> 'When it is deemed necessary' would include poor visibility during the day.

(d) The Rules concerning shapes shall be complied with by day.
(e) The lights and shapes specified in these Rules shall comply with the provisions of Annex I to these Regulations.

> Annex I covers the technical standards and spacing of lights and shapes.

COLLISION REGULATIONS HANDBOOK

Rule 21

Definitions

(a) 'Masthead light' means a white light placed over the fore and aft centreline of the vessel showing an unbroken light over an arc of the horizon of 225 degrees and so fixed as to show the light from right ahead to 22.5 degrees abaft the beam on either side of the vessel.

(b) 'Sidelights' means a green light on the starboard side and a red light on the port side each showing an unbroken light over an arc of the horizon of 112.5 degrees and so fixed as to show the light from the right ahead to 22.5 degrees abaft the beam on its respective side. In a vessel of less than 20m in length the sidelights may be combined in one lantern carried on the fore and aft centreline of the vessel.

(c) 'Sternlight' means a white light placed as nearly as practicable at the stern showing an unbroken light over an arc of the horizon of 135 degrees and so fixed as to show the light 67.5 degrees from right aft on each side of the vessel.

(d) 'Towing light' means a yellow light having the same characteristics as the 'sternlight' defined in paragraph (c) of this Rule.

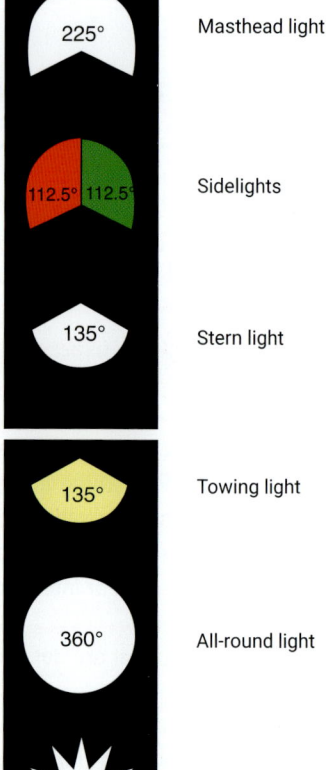

▲ Rule 21

(e) 'All-round light' means a light showing an unbroken light over an arc of the horizon of 360 degrees.

(f) 'Flashing light' means a light flashing at regular intervals at a frequency of 120 flashes or more per minute.

> Flashing lights would commonly be for an air-cushion vessel (yellow) or WIG (red)
> Note also that flashing lights are also commonly fitted on various navies' submarines, but they will not necessarily flash at the frequency stipulated in this Rule. See NP 100 *The Mariner's Handbook* for further details.
> Blue flashing lights could be displayed by law enforcement (police, customs, border force) and RNLI vessels.

PART C – LIGHTS AND SHAPES

Rule 22

Visibility of lights

The lights prescribed in these Rules shall have an intensity as specified in Section 8 of Annex I to these Regulations so as to be visible at the following minimum ranges:
(a) In vessels of 50m or more in length:
- a masthead light, 6 miles;
- a sidelight, 3 miles;
- a sternlight, 3 miles;
- a towing light, 3 miles;
- a white, red, green or yellow all-round light, 3 miles.

(b) In vessels of 12m or more in length but less than 50m in length:
- a masthead light, 5 miles; except that where the length of the vessel is less than 20m, 3 miles;
- a sidelight, 2 miles;
- a sternlight, 2 miles;
- a towing light, 2 miles;
- a white, red, green or yellow all-round light, 2 miles.

(c) In vessels of less than 12m in length:
- a masthead light, 2 miles;
- a sidelight, 1 mile;
- a sternlight, 2 miles;
- a towing light, 2 miles
- a white, red, green or yellow all-round light, 2 miles.

(d) In inconspicuous, partly submerged vessels or objects being towed:
- a white all-round light, 3 miles.

Rule 22 Visibility of Lights				*numbers are Nautical Miles	
Light	Colour	Placement	>50m	50-12m	<12m
Masthead light	White	Centreline	6	5 (3 if <20m)	2
Sidelight	Red or green	On or close to the side	3	2	1
Sternlight	White	On or close to the stern	3	2	2
Towing light	Yellow	Close to the stern	3	2	2
All-round light	White, red, green, yellow	Where best seen	3	2	2

COLLISION REGULATIONS HANDBOOK

> Note: Special attention should be paid to the fact that some vessels alter their lights depending on whether they are underway or making way. The definition given in Rule 3(i) of underway is 'a vessel is not at anchor, or made fast to the shore, or aground'. We could further consider that the vessel would be drifting with the stream and wind. However, there is no definition of making way, but by process of elimination this would mean being actively propelled on her course by machinery, sails or oars.

Rule 23

Power-driven vessels underway

▼ Rule 23(a)

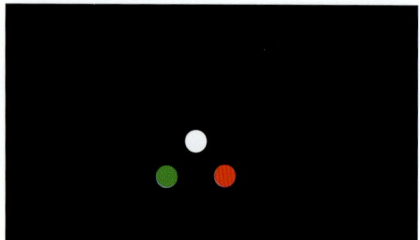

- Power-driven vessel less than 50m
- Underway

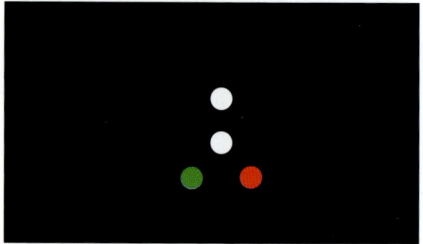

- Power-driven vessel probably over 50m
- Ahead
- Underway

(a) A power-driven vessel underway shall exhibit:
  (i) a masthead light forward;
  (ii) a second masthead light abaft of and higher than the forward one; except that a vessel of less than 50m in length shall not be obliged to exhibit such light but may do so;
  (iii) sidelights;
  (iv) a sternlight.

▼ Rule 23(b)

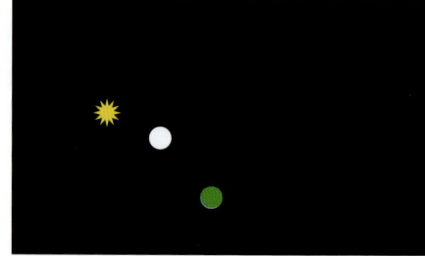

- Air cushion vehicle
- Less than 50m
- Non-displacement mode
- Starboard side

(b) An air-cushion vessel when operating in the non-displacement mode shall, in addition to the lights prescribed in paragraph (a) of this Rule, exhibit an all-round flashing yellow light.

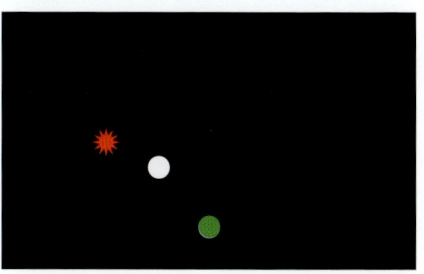

◀ Rule 23(c)

- WIG
- Less than 50m
- When taking off, landing or flying at surface
- Starboard side

(c) A WIG craft only when taking off, landing and in flight near the surface shall, in addition to the lights prescribed in paragraph (a) of this Rule, exhibit a high intensity all-round flashing red light.

(d)
    (i) a power-driven vessel of less than 12m in length may in lieu of the lights prescribed in paragraph (a) of this Rule exhibit an all-round white light and sidelights;

> Therefore, instead of separate stern and masthead white lights, an all-round white light can be used on a vessel less than 12m.

    (ii) a power-driven vessel of less than 7m in length whose maximum speed does not exceed 7 knots may in lieu of the lights prescribed in paragraph (a) of this Rule exhibit an all-round white light and shall, if practicable, also exhibit sidelights;

> It needs to comply with both under 7m and with a maximum speed of less than 7 knots to only show an all-round white light.

    (iii) the masthead light or all-round white light on a power-driven vessel of less than 12m in length may be displaced from the fore and aft centreline of the vessel if centreline fitting is not practicable, provided that the sidelights are combined in one lantern which shall be carried on the fore and aft centreline of the vessel or located as nearly as practicable in the same fore and aft line as the masthead light or the all-round white light.

> An instance where this may arise is on a small fishing vessel that has its cabin offset to one side of the boat to give a clear working deck on the other side.

Rule 24

Towing and pushing

▼ Rule 24(a)

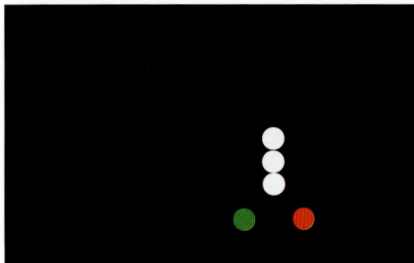

- Vessel towing
- Under 50m
- Ahead
- Towing more than 200m

▼ Rule 24(a)

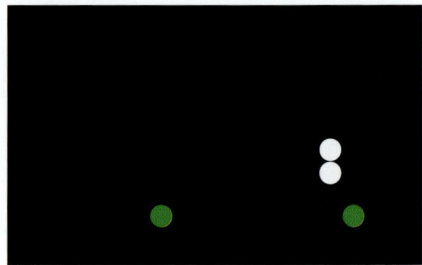

- Vessel towing
- Under 50m
- Starboard aspect
- Towing less than 200m

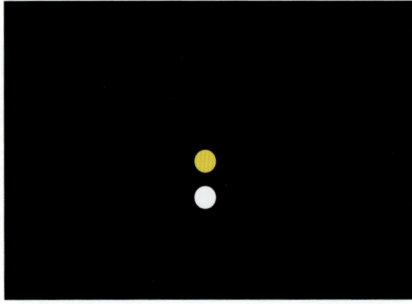

▲ Rule 24(a)(iv)

- Vessel towing
- Stern aspect
- If you see this, you are on the tow

(a) A power-driven vessel when towing shall exhibit:
  (i) instead of the light prescribed in Rule 23(a)(i) or (a)(ii), two masthead lights in a vertical line. When the length of the tow, measuring from the stern of the towing vessel to the after end of the tow exceeds 200m, three such lights in a vertical line;
  (ii) sidelights;
  (iii) a sternlight;
  (iv) a towing light in a vertical line above the sternlight;
  (v) when the length of the tow exceeds 200m, a diamond shape where it can best be seen.

PART C – LIGHTS AND SHAPES

> The day shape of a diamond is displayed on the vessel towing (tug) and shown when the length of tow exceeds 200m. Tows of less than 200m require no day shape. Towing vessels can additionally display ball-diamond-ball if they consider that they are also restricted in their ability to manoeuvre. Later on in Rule 24, Rule 24(e)(iii) states that the towed vessel also needs a diamond when the length of tow exceeds 200m.

(b) When a pushing vessel and a vessel being pushed ahead are rigidly connected in a composite unit they shall be regarded as a power-driven vessel and exhibit the lights prescribed in Rule 23.

> Therefore they just show the lights of a power-driven vessel.
>   Definitions of rigidly connected are scant. Transport Canada's interpretation is: 'The term "rigidly connected" in the *Collision Regulations* means that the connection results in there being no relative motion between the pushing vessel and the vessel being pushed ahead.'
>   The US interpretation commonly found is: 'A "composite unit" is interpreted to be the combination of a pushing vessel and a vessel being pushed ahead that are rigidly connected by mechanical means so they react to sea and swell as one vessel. Mechanical means does not include lines, wires, hawsers or chains.

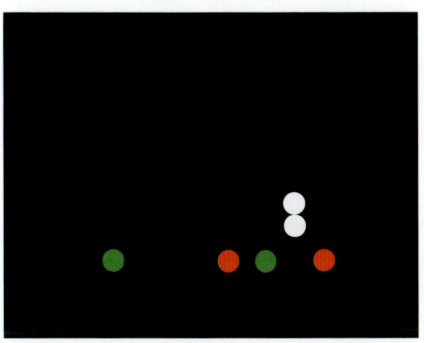

◀ Rule 24(c)

- Vessel towing
- Under 50m
- Ahead
- Towing alongside

(c) A power-driven vessel when pushing ahead or towing alongside, except in the case of a composite unit, shall exhibit:
   (i) instead of the light prescribed in Rule 23(a)(i) or (a)(ii), two masthead lights in a vertical line;
   (ii) sidelights;
   (iii) a sternlight.

COLLISION REGULATIONS HANDBOOK

Note: A tug pushing ahead or towing alongside does not show a yellow towing light aft.

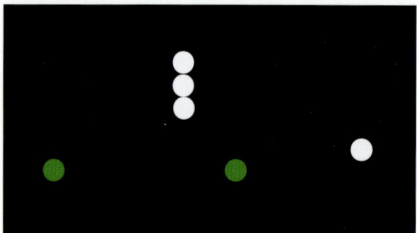

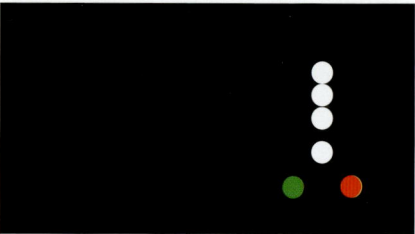

▲ Rule 24(d)
- Vessel towing
- Probably over 50m
- Starboard aspect
- Towing more than 200m

- Vessel towing
- Probably over 50m
- Ahead
- Towing more than 200m

(d) A power-driven vessel to which paragraph (a) or (c) of this Rule applies shall also comply with Rule 23(a)(ii).

If the towing vessel is over 50m, it will display another masthead light to indicate the tug's length.
 The following sections discuss what the towed object should display.

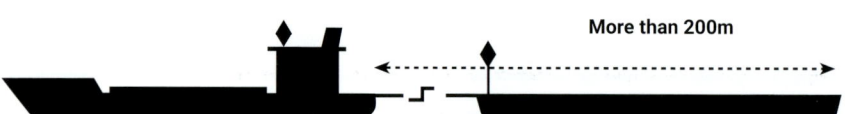

▲ Rule 24(e)

(e) A vessel or object being towed, other than those mentioned in paragraph g) of this Rule, shall exhibit:
  (i) sidelights;
  (ii) a sternlight;
  (iii) when the length of the tow exceeds 200m, a diamond shape where it can best be seen.

Note: No masthead lights are shown on the towed vessel.
 When the length of tow is over 200m, both the tug (24(a)(v)) and tow (24(d)(iii)) each exhibit a diamond day shape.

PART C – LIGHTS AND SHAPES

(f) Provided that any number of vessels being towed alongside or pushed in a group shall be lighted as one vessel,
- (i) a vessel being pushed ahead, not being part of a composite unit, shall exhibit at the forward end sidelights;
- (ii) a vessel being towed alongside shall exhibit a stern light and, at the forward end, sidelights.

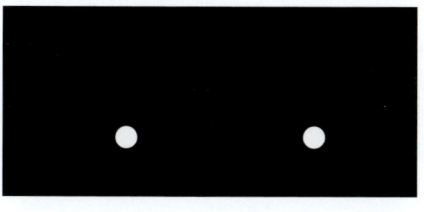

◀ Rule 24(g)(i)

- Inconspicuous, partly submerged object
- Less than 25m breadth

(g) An inconspicuous, partly submerged vessel or object, or combination of such vessels or objects being towed, shall exhibit:
- (i) if it is less than 25m in breadth, one all-round white light at or near the forward end and one at or near the after end, except that dracones need not exhibit a light at or near the forward end;

▼ Rule 24(g)(ii)

▼ Rule 24(g)(iii)

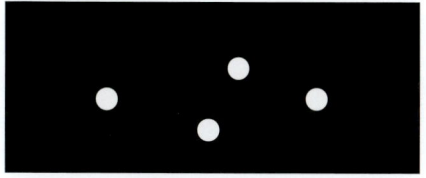

- Inconspicuous, partly submerged object
- More than 25m in breadth
- Two whites at the ends
- Two whites at the breadth

- Inconspicuous, partly submerged object
- More than 25m in breadth
- Two whites at the ends
- Two whites at the breadth
- More than 100m – white every 100m

- (ii) if it is 25m or more in breadth, two additional all-round white lights at or near the extremities of its breadth;
- (iii) if it exceeds 100m in length, additional all-round white lights between the lights prescribed in sub-paragraphs (i) and (ii) so that the distance between the lights shall not exceed 100m;

Rule 24(g)(iv) ▶

COLLISION REGULATIONS HANDBOOK

(iv) a diamond shape at or near the aftermost extremity of the last vessel or object being towed, and if the length of the tow exceeds 200m an additional diamond shape where it can best be seen and located as far forward as is practicable.

(h) Where from any sufficient cause it is impracticable for a vessel or object being towed to exhibit the lights or shapes prescribed in paragraph (e) or (g) of this Rule, all possible measures shall be taken to light the vessel or object towed or at least to indicate the presence of such vessel or object.

(i) Where from any sufficient cause it is impracticable for a vessel not normally engaged in towing operations to display the lights prescribed in paragraph (a) or (c) of this Rule, such vessel shall not be required to exhibit those lights when engaged in towing another vessel in distress or otherwise in need of assistance. All possible measures shall be taken to indicate the nature of the relationship between the towing vessel and the vessel being towed as authorized by Rule 36, in particular by illuminating the towline.

> If you take a tow at sea, but you do not have the shapes or lights described, you would do your best but at least illuminate the towline. Other things that could be done would be to inform port, harbour and routing authorities so that they could inform others. If at sea, a safety/securité message could be sent to inform other vessels.

Rule 25

Sailing vessels underway and vessels under oars

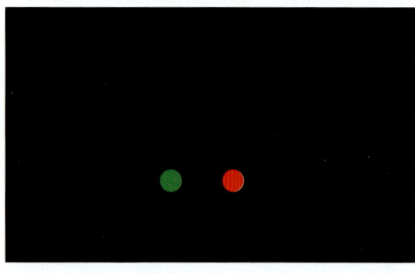

◀ Rule 25(a). Vessels under oars may display the lights for sailing vessels or those in Rule 25(d)(ii), such as a torch.

- Sailing vessel or vessel under oars
- Ahead
- No indication of length

(a) A sailing vessel underway shall exhibit:
  (i) sidelights;
  (ii) a sternlight.

PART C – LIGHTS AND SHAPES

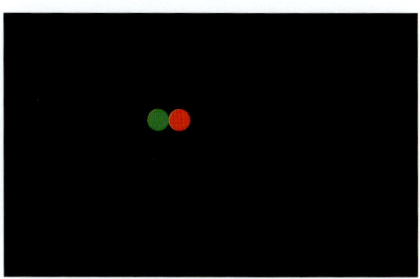

◀ Rule 25(b)

- Sailing vessel, bow aspect
- Combined in one lantern (under 20m)

(b) In a sailing vessel of less than 20m in length the lights prescribed in paragraph (a) of this Rule may be combined in one lantern carried at or near the top of the mast where it can best be seen.

> This light is often known as a tricolour light and sits on the top of the mast. Tricolour lights are very useful for sailing yachts when offshore as they only require one bulb and therefore power usage is low. Caution is advised when in port approaches where a sailing vessel's masthead tricolour may get lost in the mass of shore lights if viewed from the bridge of a larger vessel. In these cases, it is often advisable for the sailing vessel to use lower lights as these are sometimes better seen against the backdrop of the sea.

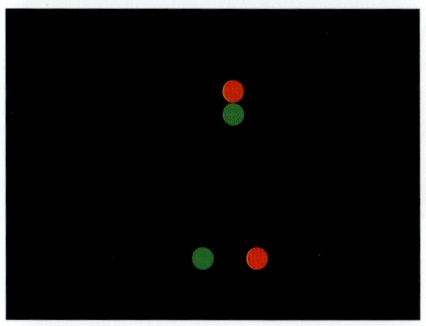

◀ Rule 25(c)

- Sailing vessel, bow aspect
- Optional lights

(c) A sailing vessel underway may, in addition to the lights prescribed in paragraph (a) of this Rule, exhibit at or near the top of the mast, where they can best be seen, two all-round lights in a vertical line, the upper being red and the lower green, but these lights shall not be exhibited in conjunction with the combined lantern permitted by paragraph (b) of this Rule.

> The additional lights at the top of the mast are often only used on larger sailing vessels.

(d)
- (i) A sailing vessel of less than 7m in length shall, if practicable, exhibit the lights prescribed in paragraph (a) or (b) of this Rule, but if she does not, she shall have ready at hand an electric torch or lighted lantern showing a white light which shall be exhibited in sufficient time to prevent collision.
- (ii) A vessel under oars may exhibit the lights prescribed in this Rule for sailing vessels, but if she does not, she shall have ready at hand an electric torch or lighted lantern showing a white light which shall be exhibited in sufficient time to prevent collision.

> While a vessel under oars is often considered a PDV, it may be lit using the lights for sailing vessels or a torch. Therefore, caution should be exercised when seeing sailing vessel lights low down as it may be either.

▲ Rule 25(e)

(e) A vessel proceeding under sail when also being propelled by machinery shall exhibit forward where it can best be seen a conical shape, apex downwards.

> This is known as motorsailing; when the sailing boat either does not have enough wind or the wind is coming from an unfavourable direction and she decides to motor as well as sail. Quite often the sailing boat will leave her mainsail up to either assist her speed or reduce rolling motion.
>
> When motorsailing with the cone, the sailing vessel becomes a power-driven vessel under the rules, and thus loses all the privileges associated with sailing.

PART C – LIGHTS AND SHAPES

Rule 26

Fishing vessels

(a) A vessel engaged in fishing, whether underway or at anchor, shall exhibit only the lights and shapes prescribed in this Rule.

> This rule applies to both vessels engaged in fishing and trawling.
> A vessel engaged in fishing at anchor does not use anchor lights.
> Vessels engaged in fishing and trawling change lights when they are underway and making way.

(b) A vessel when engaged in trawling, by which is meant the dragging through the water of a dredge net or other apparatus used as a fishing appliance, shall exhibit:

(i) two all-round lights in a vertical line, the upper being green and the lower white, or a shape consisting of two cones with their apexes together in a vertical line one above the other;

(ii) a masthead light abaft of and higher than the all-round green light; a vessel of less than 50m in length shall not be obliged to exhibit such a light but may do so;

(iii) when making way through the water, in addition to the lights prescribed in this paragraph, sidelights and a sternlight.

▼ Rule 26(b)(i), (ii) and (iii)

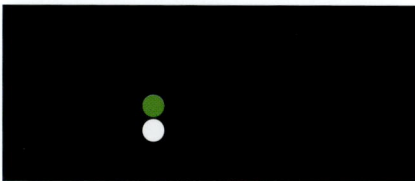

- Vessel engaged in trawling
- Less than 50m
- Underway or at anchor

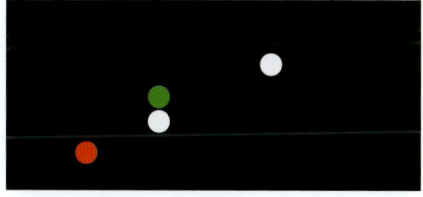

- Vessel engaged in trawling
- Port aspect
- Probably more than 50m
- Making way (addition of the sidelight)

COLLISION REGULATIONS HANDBOOK

> Vessels engaged in trawling give an indication of size at night by using a masthead light, abaft and higher than the trawling lights to show they are probably more than 50m in length. However, vessels engaged in fishing do not show such a light.

▶ Rule 26(c)(i) • Vessel engaged in fishing
• At anchor or underway

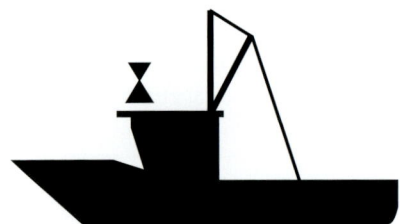

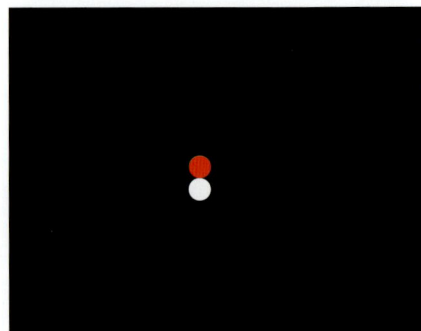

(c) A vessel engaged in fishing, other than trawling, shall exhibit:
  (i) two all-round lights in a vertical line, the upper being red and the lower white, or a shape consisting of two cones with apexes together in a vertical line one above the other;

◀ Rule 26(c)(ii). Outlying gear

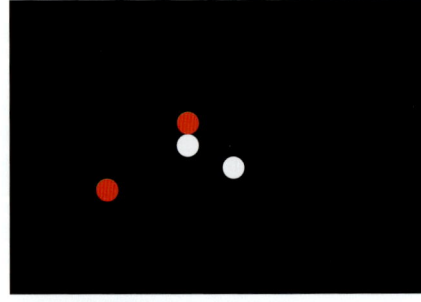

(ii) when there is outlying gear extending more than 150m horizontally from the vessel, an all-round white light or a cone apex upwards in the direction of the gear;

▲ Rule 26(c)(iii)

• Vessel engaged in fishing
• Port aspect
• Gear extending more than 150m
• Length unknown

(iii) when making way through the water, in addition to the lights prescribed in this paragraph, sidelights and a sternlight.

78

PART C – LIGHTS AND SHAPES

Unlike the vessel engaged in trawling, there are no masthead lights for vessels engaged in fishing, therefore no indication of length. An additional white light indicates outlying gear. The white light indicating outlying gear is placed 'not higher than the all-round white prescribed in 26(c)(i) and not lower than the side lights' (Annex 1(4)(a)).

(d) The additional signals described in Annex II to these Regulations apply to a vessel engaged in fishing in close proximity to other vessels engaged in fishing.

Annex II has additional lights for vessels:
- Shooting nets (two whites)
- Hauling nets (white over red)
- Nets caught on an obstruction (two reds).

(e) A vessel when not engaged in fishing shall not exhibit the lights or shapes prescribed in this Rule, but only those prescribed for a vessel of her length.

This is often abused and many fishing vessels have the shapes welded in place and identification lights permanently on.

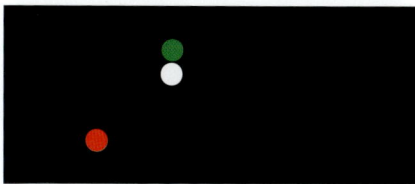

- Vessel engaged in trawling, underway and making way
- Port aspect
- Less than 50m

- Vessel engaged in fishing, underway and making way
- Purse seiner hampered by nets
- Port aspect
- Yellow lights are alternate and flashing

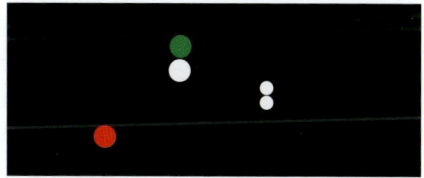

- Vessel engaged in trawling, underway and making way
- Port aspect
- Less than 50m
- Shooting nets
- (See Annex II)

COLLISION REGULATIONS HANDBOOK

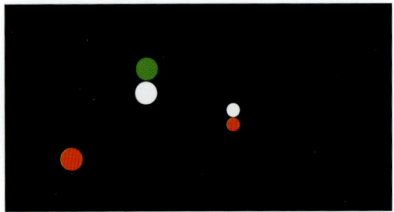

- Vessel engaged in trawling, underway and making way
- Port aspect
- Less than 50m
- Hauling nets
- (See Annex II)

- Vessel engaged in trawling
- Port aspect
- Less than 50m
- Nets fast
- (See Annex II)

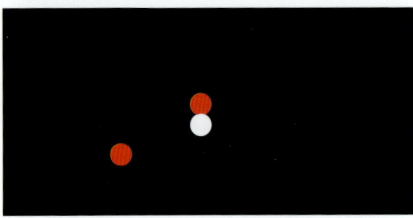

- Vessel engaged in fishing, underway and making way
- Port aspect

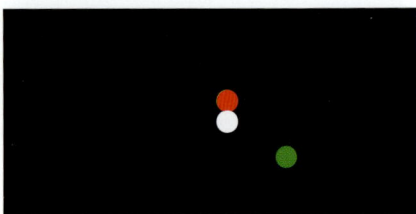

- Vessel engaged in fishing, underway and making way
- Starboard aspect

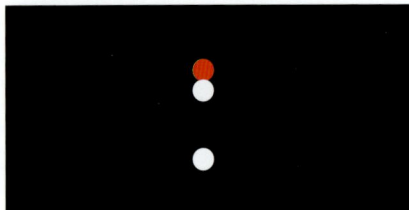

- Vessel engaged in fishing, underway and making way
- Stern aspect
- Or possibly not making way, but with outlying gear

Rule 27

Vessels not under command or restricted in their ability to manoeuvre

With both NUC and RAM, there is a change of lights when starting to make way – while still displaying their two reds or red-white-red. A vessel NUC changes her sidelights and sternlight and ensures her masthead lights are switched off so that, from certain aspects, she cannot be mistaken for a vessel aground. A vessel RAM changes sidelights, sternlight and masthead light.

PART C – LIGHTS AND SHAPES

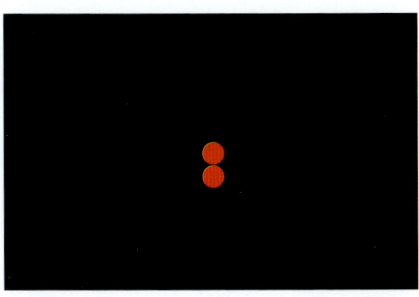

◄ Rule 27(a)(i)

- Not under command
- Unknown aspect
- Underway

◄ Rule 27(a)(ii)

- Not under command – day shape of two black balls.

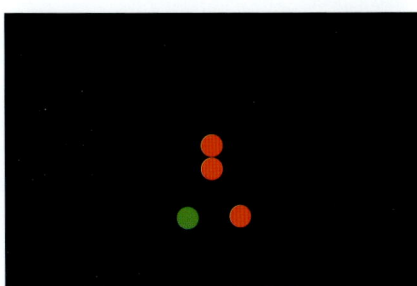

◄ Rule 27 a)(iii)

- Not under command
- Ahead aspect
- Underway and making way

(a) A vessel not under command shall exhibit:
  (i) two all-round red lights in a vertical line where they can best be seen;
  (ii) two balls or similar shapes in a vertical line where they can best be seen;
  (iii) when making way through the water, in addition to the lights prescribed in this paragraph, sidelights and a sternlight.

(b) A vessel restricted in her ability to manoeuvre, except a vessel engaged in mine clearance operations, shall exhibit:
  (i) three all-round lights in a vertical line where they can best be seen. The highest and lowest of these lights shall be red and the middle light shall be white;
  (ii) three shapes in a vertical line where they can best be seen. The highest and lowest of these shapes shall be balls and the middle one a diamond;

COLLISION REGULATIONS HANDBOOK

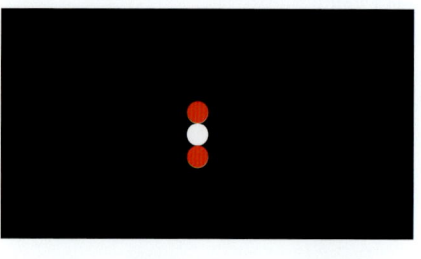

◀ Rule 27(b)(i)

• Restricted in ability to manoeuvre

◀ Rule 27(b)(ii)

• Restricted in ability to manoeuvre
• Day shape
• Ball-diamond-ball

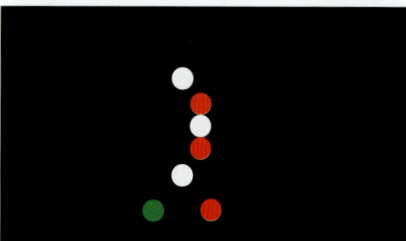

◀ Rule 27(b)(iii)

• Restricted in ability to manoeuvre
• Making way
• Probably over 50m
• Ahead aspect

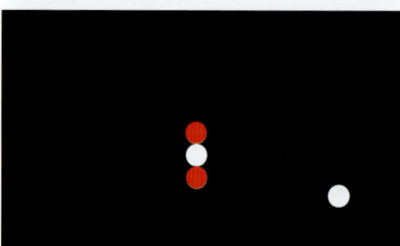

◀ Rule 27(b)(iv)

• Restricted in ability to manoeuvre
• At anchor (or making way if seen from astern)
• If at anchor, less than 50m
• If making way, no indication of length

(iii) when making way through the water, a masthead light or lights, sidelights and a sternlight, in addition to the lights prescribed in sub-paragraph (i);

Note: There is a change of lights when making way.

(iv) when at anchor, in addition to the lights or shapes prescribed in sub-paragraphs (i) and (ii), the light, lights or shape prescribed in Rule 30.

(c) A power-driven vessel engaged in a towing operation such as severely restricts the towing vessel and her tow in their ability to deviate from their course shall, in addition

PART C – LIGHTS AND SHAPES

to the lights or shapes prescribed in Rule 24(a), exhibit the lights or shapes prescribed in sub-paragraphs (b)(i) and (ii) of this Rule.

> Therefore, if a towing vessel is severely restricted by the tow she must show both towing lights and those of RAM. While a towing vessel might not be severely restricted in open sea, she may become so when entering or exiting coastal and harbour waters.

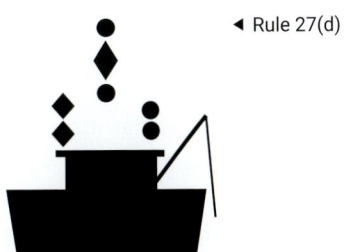

◄ Rule 27(d)

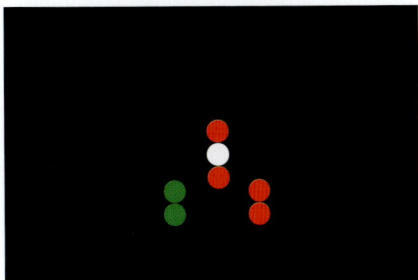

- Restricted in ability to manoeuvre
- Obstruction on red side
- Unknown aspect

(d) A vessel engaged in dredging or underwater operations, when restricted in her ability to manoeuvre, shall exhibit the lights and shapes prescribed in sub-paragraphs (b)(i), (ii) and (iii) of this Rule and shall in addition, when an obstruction exists, exhibit:
  (i) two all-round red lights or two balls in a vertical line to indicate the side on which the obstruction exists;
  (ii) two all-round green lights or two diamonds in a vertical line to indicate the side on which another vessel may pass;
  (iii) when at anchor, the lights or shapes prescribed in this paragraph instead of the lights or shape prescribed in Rule 30.

> At anchor, there is a change in lights between a standard RAM and a RAM that is engaged in dredging or underwater operations.

COLLISION REGULATIONS HANDBOOK

> The standard RAM displays RAM lights/shapes and anchor lights/shapes, whereas the RAM dredger, etc. just displays her RAM plus two greens and reds and by day ball-diamond-ball, then ball-ball/diamond-diamond.

(e) Whenever the size of a vessel engaged in diving operations makes it impracticable to exhibit all lights and shapes prescribed in paragraph (d) of this Rule, the following shall be exhibited:

(i) three all-round lights in a vertical line where they can best be seen. The highest and lowest of these lights shall be red and the middle light shall be white;

▲ Rule 27(e)(ii)

(ii) a rigid replica of the International Code flag 'A' not less than 1m in height. Measures shall be taken to ensure its all-round visibility.

> Therefore, the Code flag 'A' is only flown (for the ColRegs) when the size of the vessel engaged in diving operations is too small to show the full-sized shapes. This is because, reading further into the positioning of lights in Annex I, Section 4, it states that the extra balls and diamonds each need to be 2m horizontally away from the RAM ball diamond ball – thus requiring the whole ensemble to be approximately 5m between one side and the other.
>
> Note the A flag is 1m in height and rigid – so not a material flag but a board or series of boards placed on the vessel to ensure visibility. A good day for diving is a calm day – not a day to fly a flag.
>
> Even if the vessel is large and does not need to fly the code flag for ColRegs compliance, they may fly it as it is good seamanship.

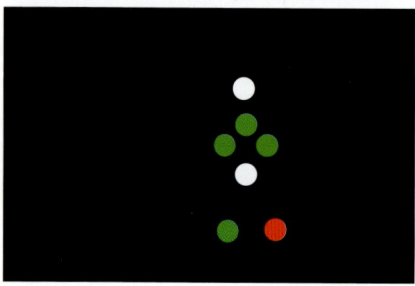

▲ Rule 27(f)

- Power-driven vessel probably over 50m
- Ahead
- Underway
- Minesweeping
- Keep away 1000m

PART C – LIGHTS AND SHAPES

(f) A vessel engaged in mine clearance operations shall in addition to the lights prescribed for a power-driven vessel in Rule 23 or to the lights or shape prescribed for a vessel at anchor in Rule 30 as appropriate, exhibit three all-round green lights or three balls. One of these lights or shapes shall be exhibited near the foremast head and one at each end of the fore yard. These lights or shapes indicate that it is dangerous for another vessel to approach within 1000m of the mine clearance vessel.

Hence, the three greens are in addition to those of a power-driven vessel or a vessel at anchor. Similar to a PDV's lights, there would be no indication if the vessel is making way.

(g) Vessels of less than 12m in length, except those engaged in diving operations, shall not be required to exhibit the lights and shapes prescribed in this Rule.

(h) The signals prescribed in this Rule are not signals of vessels in distress and requiring assistance. Such signals are contained in Annex IV to these Regulations.

Rule 28

Vessels constrained by their draught

A vessel constrained by her draught may, in addition to the lights prescribed for power-driven vessels in Rule 23, exhibit where they can best be seen three all-round red lights in a vertical line, or a cylinder.

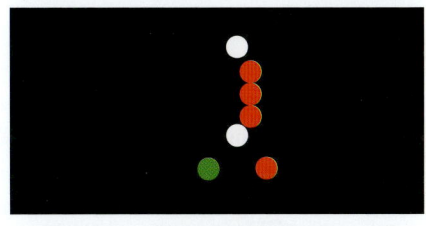

▲ Rule 28
- Constrained by draught
- Probably over 50m
- Ahead aspect
- Underway

- Constrained by draught – cylinder by day

85

Rule 29

Pilot vessels

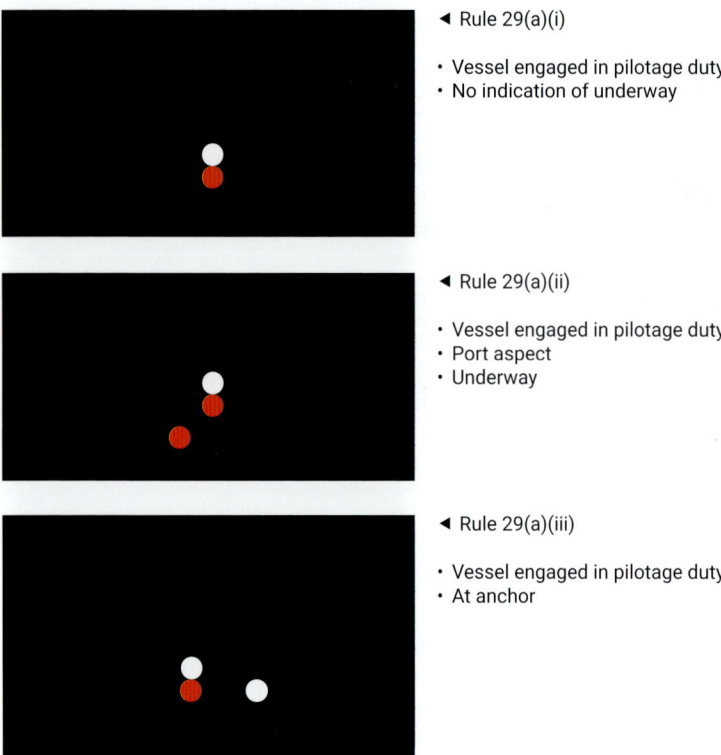

◀ Rule 29(a)(i)

- Vessel engaged in pilotage duty
- No indication of underway

◀ Rule 29(a)(ii)

- Vessel engaged in pilotage duty
- Port aspect
- Underway

◀ Rule 29(a)(iii)

- Vessel engaged in pilotage duty
- At anchor

(a) A vessel engaged on pilotage duty shall exhibit:
   (i) at or near the masthead, two all-round lights in a vertical line, the upper being white and the lower red;
   (ii) when underway, in addition, sidelights and a sternlight;
   (iii) when at anchor, in addition to the lights prescribed in sub-paragraph (i), the light, lights or shape prescribed in Rule 30 for vessels at anchor.

(b) A pilot vessel when not engaged on pilotage duty shall exhibit the lights or shapes prescribed for a similar vessel of her length.

> Note: No masthead lights when underway on pilotage duty.

PART C – LIGHTS AND SHAPES

Rule 30

Anchored vessels and vessels aground

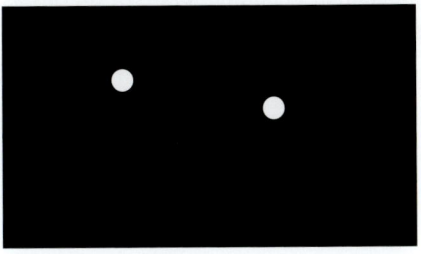

◀ Rule 30(a), (b) and (c)

- At anchor over 50m
- High light near the bow
- Port aspect

- At anchor over 50m
- High light near the bow
- May show deck lights but will show deck lights over 100m
- Port aspect

(a) A vessel at anchor shall exhibit where it can best be seen:
  (i) in the fore part, an all-round white light or one ball;
  (ii) at or near the stern and at a lower level than the light prescribed in sub-paragraph (i), an all-round white light.

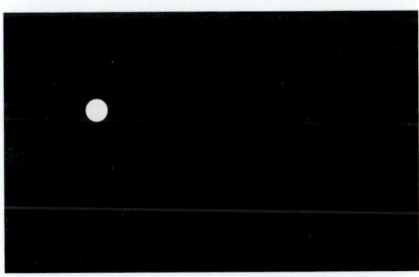

▲ Be aware that a single white could be a vessel under 50m at anchor or a sailing vessel under 7m, vessel under oars or a power-driven vessel less than 7m and 7 knots

(b) A vessel of less than 50m in length may exhibit an all-round white light where it can best be seen instead of the lights prescribed in paragraph (a) of this Rule.

(c) A vessel at anchor may, and a vessel of 100m and more in length shall, also use the available working or equivalent lights to illuminate her decks.

COLLISION REGULATIONS HANDBOOK

> Note: The forward light is now the high light when at anchor, whereas when a PDV is underway the forward light is the lower of the two whites.

(d) A vessel aground shall exhibit the lights prescribed in paragraph (a) or (b) of this Rule and in addition, where they can best be seen:

(i) two all-round red lights in a vertical line;

(ii) three balls in a vertical line.

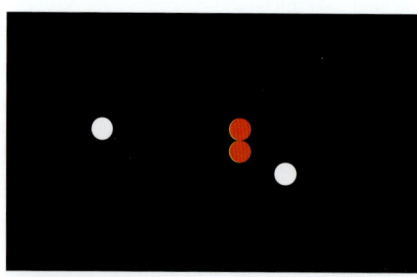

▲ Rule 30(d)
- Aground
- Probably over 50m

(e) A vessel of less than 7m in length, when at anchor, not in or near a narrow channel, fairway or anchorage, or where other vessels normally navigate, shall not be required to exhibit the lights or shape prescribed in paragraphs (a) and (b) of this Rule.

> Small vessels under 7m need show no lights or shapes, so long as they are anchored out of the way.

▲ Rule 30(d)(ii)

- Aground – three balls

Rule 31

Seaplanes

Where it is impracticable for a seaplane or a WIG craft to exhibit lights and shapes of the characteristics or in the positions prescribed in the Rules of this Part, she shall exhibit lights and shapes as closely similar in characteristics and position as is possible.

(f) A vessel of less than 12m in length, when aground, shall not be required to exhibit the lights or shapes prescribed in sub-paragraphs (d)(i) and (ii) of this Rule.

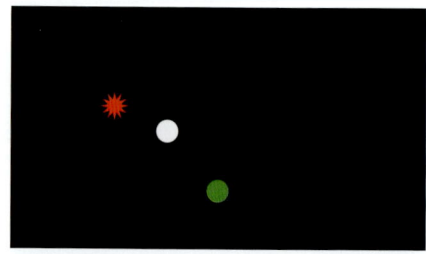

▲ Rule 31
- WIG
- Less than 50m
- When taking off, landing or flying at surface
- Starboard side

PART C – LIGHTS AND SHAPES

Vessels that change lights between underway and making way

Vessel	Underway	Making way	Notes
Power-driven vessel	PDV lights	Same	
Air-cushion vessel	PDV plus flashing yellow	Same	
WIG	PDV plus flashing red	Same	
Tug	PDV plus towing lights	Same	
Sailing	Sail lights	Same	
Trawling	All-round lights G/W plus masthead if over 50m	Sidelights and sternlight	Underway lights used at anchor (no anchor light)
Fishing	All-round lights R/W – no indication of length	Sidelights and sternlight	Underway lights used at anchor (no anchor light)
NUC	All-round lights R/R	Sidelights and sternlight	
RAM	All-round lights R/W/R. Doesn't state underway, changes when making way	Masthead, sidelights and sternlight	At anchor: all-round lights and anchor lights
RAM, towing	All-round lights R/W/R plus lights used in tow	Same	
RAM, dredge, UW ops	All-round lights R/W/R plus R/R G/G	Same	Underway lights used at anchor (no anchor light)
Mine clearance	PDV plus G/G/G	Same	Anchor plus G/G/G
CBD	PDV plus all-round lights R/R/R	Same	
Pilot	If engaged in pilotage duties and even if not underway W/R. When underway sidelights and a sternlight	Same	All-round lights W/R plus anchor lights

89

PART D – SOUND AND LIGHT SIGNALS

Rule 32

When reading through this Part, special care should be taken to check when a sound signal is made; for instance, manoeuvring signals are NOT sounded in restricted visibility.

Definitions

(a) The word 'whistle' means any sound signalling appliance capable of producing the prescribed blasts and which complies with the specifications in Annex III to these Regulations.
(b) The term 'short blast' means a blast of about one second's duration.
(c) The term 'prolonged blast' means a blast of from four to six seconds' duration.

Note: The word 'whistle' also means ship's horn.

Rule 33

Equipment for sound signals

(a) A vessel of 12m or more in length shall be provided with a whistle, a vessel of 20m or more in length shall be provided with a bell in addition to a whistle, and a vessel of 100m or more in length shall, in addition, be provided with a gong, the tone and sound of which cannot be confused with that of the bell. The whistle, bell and gong shall comply with the specifications in Annex III to these Regulations. The bell or gong or both may be replaced by other equipment having the same respective sound characteristics, provided that manual sounding of the prescribed signals shall always be possible.

COLLISION REGULATIONS HANDBOOK

Sound signalling equipment	
Size of Vessel	Carriage
Less than 12m	Either whistle and bell or other means to make an efficient sound signal
12m or more	Whistle
20m or more	Whistle and bell
100m or more	Whistle, bell and gong

(b) A vessel of less than 12m in length shall not be obliged to carry the sound signalling appliances prescribed in paragraph (a) of this Rule but if she does not, she shall be provided with some other means of making an efficient sound signal.

Rule 34

Manoeuvring and warning signals

(a) When vessels are in sight of one another, a power-driven vessel underway, when manoeuvring as authorized or required by these Rules, shall indicate that manoeuvre by the following signals on her whistle:
- one short blast to mean 'I am altering my course to starboard';
- two short blasts to mean 'I am altering my course to port';
- three short blasts to mean 'I am operating astern propulsion'.

> These signals are for when vessels are in sight of one another, therefore they would not be used in restricted visibility or any action taken in compliance with Rule 19.
>
> These signals would only be given by a PDV underway when manoeuvring. Therefore, any manoeuvre to avoid a collision when in sight of another vessel should be preceded by the appropriate sound signal. However, you are not obliged to make those signals if you are a vessel engaged in fishing, sailing, etc.

(b) Any vessel may supplement the whistle signals prescribed in paragraph (a) of this Rule by light signals, repeated as appropriate, whilst the manoeuvre is being carried out:
  (i) these light signals shall have the following significance:
  - one flash to mean 'I am altering my course to starboard';

PART D – SOUND AND LIGHT SIGNALS

- two flashes to mean 'I am altering my course to port';
- three flashes to mean 'I am operating astern propulsion';

> 'Supplement' is defined as 'a thing that is added to something else to improve or complete it' (*Oxford Learner's Dictionaries*). Therefore, the light signals would be in addition to sound signals.

(ii) the duration of each flash shall be about one second, the interval between flashes shall be about one second, and the interval between successive signals shall be not less than ten seconds;

(iii) the light used for this signal shall, if fitted, be an all-round white light, visible at a minimum range of 5 miles, and shall comply with the provisions of Annex I to these Regulations.

> In the following rules, the sound signals can be used by any vessel.

(c) When in sight of one another in a narrow channel or fairway:

> This rule indicates when in a 'narrow channel or fairway', therefore not when overtaking on the open sea.

(i) a vessel intending to overtake another shall in compliance with Rule 9(e)(i) indicate her intention by the following signals on her whistle:
- two prolonged blasts followed by one short blast to mean 'I intend to overtake you on your starboard side';

▬▬ ▬▬ ●

- two prolonged blasts followed by two short blasts to mean 'I intend to overtake you on your port side'.

▬▬ ▬▬ ● ●

(ii) the vessel about to be overtaken when acting in accordance with Rule 9(e)(i) shall indicate her agreement by the following signal on her whistle:
- one prolonged, one short, one prolonged and one short blast, in that order.

▬▬ ● ▬▬ ●

> Long-short-long-short is also the Morse code for Charlie, which is 'Yes'.

(d) When vessels in sight of one another are approaching each other and from any cause either vessel fails to understand the intentions or actions of the other, or is in doubt whether sufficient action is being taken by the other to avoid collision, the vessel in doubt shall immediately indicate such doubt by giving at least five short and rapid blasts on the whistle. Such signal may be supplemented by a light signal of at least five short and rapid flashes.

● ● ● ● ●

(e) A vessel nearing a bend or an area of a channel or fairway where other vessels may be obscured by an intervening obstruction shall sound one prolonged blast. Such signal shall be answered with a prolonged blast by any approaching vessel that may be within hearing around the bend or behind the intervening obstruction.

> Note: Rule 34(e) is the only part in this Rule where it does NOT state that vessels must be in sight of one another; therefore, it could also be used in restricted visibility when nearing a bend in a fairway or channel. It can also be used by any vessel.

(f) If whistles are fitted on a vessel at a distance apart of more than 100m, one whistle only shall be used for giving manoeuvring and warning signals.

> This is so that, due to the velocity of sound, signals from two separate sources do not arrive at the listener at different times. For example, if using two widely separated whistles, one short blast could be heard as two.

Rule 35

Sound signals in restricted visibility

In or near an area of restricted visibility, whether by day or night, the signals prescribed in this Rule shall be used as follows:

PART D – SOUND AND LIGHT SIGNALS

(a) A power-driven vessel making way through the water shall sound at intervals of not more than 2 minutes one prolonged blast.

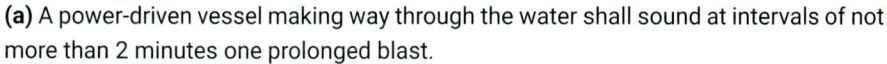

(b) A power-driven vessel underway but stopped and making no way through the water shall sound at intervals of not more than 2 minutes two prolonged blasts in succession with an interval of about 2 seconds between them.

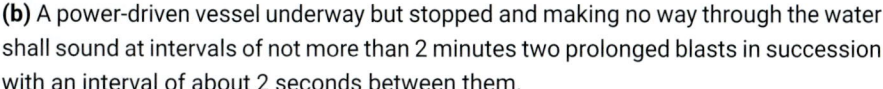

(c) A vessel not under command, a vessel restricted in her ability to manoeuvre, a vessel constrained by her draught, a sailing vessel, a vessel engaged in fishing and a vessel engaged in towing or pushing another vessel shall, instead of the signals prescribed in paragraphs (a) or (b) of this Rule, sound at intervals of not more than 2 minutes three blasts in succession, namely one prolonged followed by two short blasts.

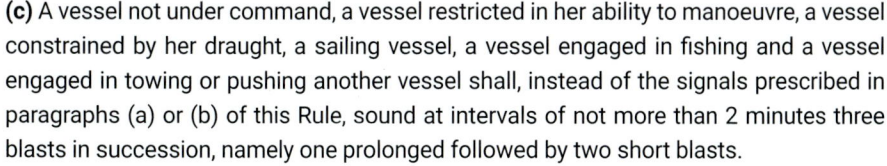

(d) A vessel engaged in fishing, when at anchor, and a vessel restricted in her ability to manoeuvre when carrying out her work at anchor, shall instead of the signals prescribed in paragraph (g) of this Rule sound the signal prescribed in paragraph (c) of this Rule.

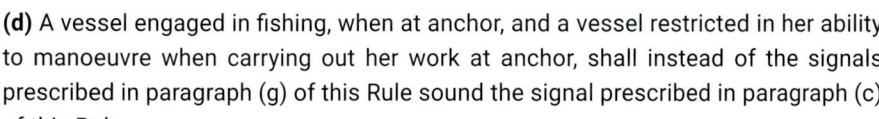

> This is one of those little idiosyncrasies where RAM and fishing vessels, when at anchor, sound one long and two short, instead of anchor signals.

(e) A vessel towed or if more than one vessel is towed the last vessel of the tow, if manned, shall at intervals of not more than 2 minutes sound four blasts in succession, namely one prolonged followed by three short blasts. When practicable, this signal shall be made immediately after the signal made by the towing vessel.

(f) When a pushing vessel and a vessel being pushed ahead are rigidly connected in a composite unit they shall be regarded as a power-driven vessel and shall give the signals prescribed in paragraphs (a) or (b) of this Rule.

COLLISION REGULATIONS HANDBOOK

> Therefore, they would be considered a power-driven vessel.

(g) A vessel at anchor shall at intervals of not more than one minute ring the bell rapidly for about 5 seconds. In a vessel of 100m or more in length the bell shall be sounded in the forepart of the vessel and immediately after the ringing of the 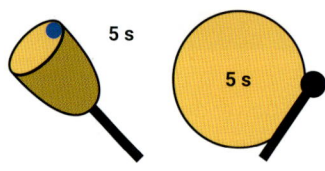 bell the gong shall be sounded rapidly for about 5 seconds in the after part of the vessel. A vessel at anchor may in addition sound three blasts in succession, namely one short, one prolonged and one short blast, to give warning of her position and of the possibility of collision to an approaching vessel.

> Vessels underway and making way will sound at intervals not exceeding 2 minutes, whereas when at anchor or aground it is *usually* at intervals not exceeding 1 minute.

(h) A vessel aground shall give the bell signal and if required the gong signal prescribed in paragraph (g) of this Rule and shall, in addition, give three separate and distinct strokes on the bell immediately before and after the rapid ringing of the bell. A vessel aground may in addition sound an appropriate whistle signal.

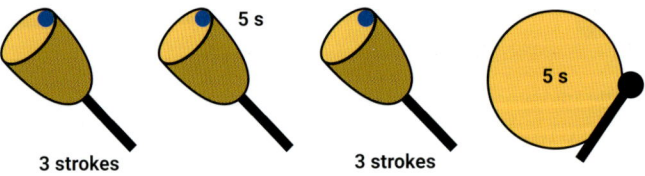

> An appropriate whistle signal for a vessel aground might be Uniform – You are running into danger:
>
>

> Intervals go back to 2 minutes now for smaller vessels.

(i) A vessel of 12m or more but less than 20m in length shall not be obliged to give the bell signals prescribed in paragraphs (g) and (h) of this Rule. However, if she does not,

PART D – SOUND AND LIGHT SIGNALS

she shall make some other efficient sound signal at intervals of not more than 2 minutes.

(j) A vessel of less than 12m in length shall not be obliged to give the above-mentioned signals but, if she does not, shall make some other efficient sound signal at intervals of not more than 2 minutes.

(k) A pilot vessel when engaged on pilotage duty may in addition to the signals prescribed in paragraphs (a), (b) or (g) of this Rule sound an identity signal consisting of four short blasts.

> Four short blasts could therefore follow, one long, two long or anchor signals.

Rule 36

Signals to attract attention

If necessary to attract the attention of another vessel any vessel may make light or sound signals that cannot be mistaken for any signal authorised elsewhere in these Rules, or may direct the beam of her searchlight in the direction of the danger, in such a way as not to embarrass any vessel. Any light to attract the attention of another vessel shall be such that it cannot be mistaken for any aid to navigation. For the purpose of this Rule, the use of high intensity intermittent or revolving lights, such as strobe lights, shall be avoided.

> An example of this is a sailing vessel that might shine a light on her sails if she believes she has not been seen. This illuminates the sails, increasing her visibility while not 'embarrassing the other vessel'.

Rule 37

Distress signals

When a vessel is in distress and requires assistance, she shall use or exhibit the signals described in Annex IV to these Regulations.

PART E – EXEMPTIONS

Rule 38

Exemptions

Any vessel (or class of vessels) provided that she complies with the requirements of the International Regulations for Preventing Collisions at Sea, 1960, the keel of which is laid or which is at a corresponding stage of construction before the entry into force of these Regulations may be exempted from compliance therewith as follows:

(a) The installation of lights with ranges prescribed in Rule 22, until 4 years after the date of entry into force of these Regulations.

(b) The installation of lights with colour specifications as prescribed in Section 7 of Annex I to these Regulations, until 4 years after the date of entry into force of these Regulations.

(c) The repositioning of lights as a result of conversion from Imperial to metric units and rounding off measurement figures, permanent exemption.

- (i) The repositioning of masthead lights on vessels of less than 150m in length, resulting from the prescriptions of Section 3(a) of Annex I to these Regulations, permanent exemption.
- (ii) The repositioning of masthead lights on vessels of 150m or more in length, resulting from the prescriptions of Section 3(a) of Annex I to these Regulations, until 9 years after the date of entry into force of these Regulations.

(d) The repositioning of masthead lights resulting from the prescriptions of Section 2(b) of Annex I to these Regulations, until 9 years after the date of entry into force of these Regulations.

(e) The repositioning of sidelights resulting from the prescriptions of Sections 2(g) and 3(b) of Annex I to these Regulations, until 9 years after the date of entry into force of these Regulations.

(f) The requirements for sound signal appliances prescribed in Annex III to these Regulations, until 9 years after the date of entry into force of these Regulations.

(g) The repositioning of all-round lights resulting from the prescription of Section 9(b) of Annex I to these Regulations, permanent exemption.

(h) The repositioning of all-round lights resulting from the prescription of Section 9(b) of Annex I to these Regulations, permanent exemption.

See Cmnd.2956 and Schedule I to the Collision Regulations (Ships and Seaplanes on the Water) and Signals of Distress (Ships) Order 1965 (S.I. 1965/1525).

PART F

Verification of compliance with the provisions of the Convention

> This section just discusses how the IMO will audit each maritime authority or government on the implementation of ColRegs.

Rule 39

Definitions

(a) Audit means a systematic, independent and documented process for obtaining audit evidence and evaluating it objectively to determine the extent to which audit criteria are fulfilled.

(b) Audit Scheme means the IMO Member State Audit Scheme established by the Organization and taking into account the guidelines developed by the Organization.

(c) Code for Implementation means the IMO Instruments Implementation Code (III Code) adopted by the Organization by resolution A.1070(28).

> IMO Instruments Implementation Code (III Code) describes how governments would implement IMO regulations and conventions within their country and on their ships.

(d) Audit Standard means the Code for Implementation.

Rule 40

Application

Contracting Parties shall use the provisions of the Code for Implementation in the execution of their obligations and responsibilities contained in the present Convention.

Rule 41

Verification of compliance

(a) Every Contracting Party shall be subject to periodic audits by the Organization in accordance with the audit standard to verify compliance with and implementation of the present Convention.

(b) The Secretary-General of the Organization shall have responsibility for administering the Audit Scheme, based on the guidelines developed by the Organization.

(c) Every Contracting Party shall have responsibility for facilitating the conduct of the audit and implementation of a programme of actions to address the findings, based on the guidelines developed by the Organization.

▲ IMO Office in London

(d) Audit of all Contracting Parties shall be: based on an overall schedule developed by the Secretary-General of the Organization, taking into account the guidelines developed by the Organization; and conducted at periodic intervals, taking into account the guidelines developed by the Organization.

ANNEX I

Positioning and technical details of lights and shapes

1. Definition

The term 'height above the hull' means height above the uppermost continuous deck. This height shall be measured from the position vertically beneath the location of the light.

2. Vertical positioning and spacing of lights

(a) On a power-driven vessel of 20m or more in length the masthead lights shall be placed as follows:
   (i) the forward masthead light, or if only one masthead light is carried, then that light, at a height above the hull of not less than 6m, and, if the breadth of the vessel exceeds 6m, then at a height above the hull not less than such breadth, so however that the light need not be placed at a greater height above the hull than 12m;
   (ii) when two masthead lights are carried the after one shall be at least 4.5m vertically higher than the forward one.

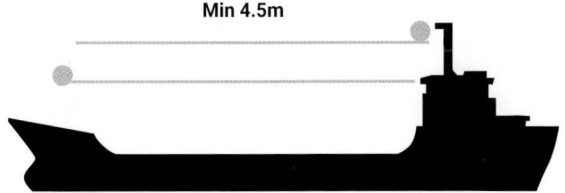

◄ Minimum vertical spacing of lights of 4.5m when two masthead lights are carried

COLLISION REGULATIONS HANDBOOK

(b) The vertical separation of masthead lights of power-driven vessels shall be such that in all normal conditions of trim the after light will be seen over and separate from the forward light at a distance of 1,000m from the stem when viewed from sea-level.

(c) The masthead light of a power-driven vessel of 12m but less than 20m in length shall be placed at a height above the gunwale of not less than 2.5m.

(d) A power-driven vessel of less than 12m in length may carry the uppermost light at a height of less than 2.5m above the gunwale. When, however, a masthead light is carried in addition to sidelights and a sternlight or the all-round light prescribed in Rule 23(c)(i) is carried in addition to sidelights, then such masthead light or all-round light shall be carried at least 1m higher than the sidelights.

(e) One of the two or three masthead lights prescribed for a power-driven vessel when engaged in towing or pushing another vessel shall be placed in the same position as either the forward masthead light or the after masthead light; provided that, if carried on the after mast, the lowest after masthead light shall be at least 4.5m vertically higher than the forward masthead light.

(f)
   (i) The masthead light or lights prescribed in Rule 23(a) shall be so placed as to be above and clear of all other lights and obstructions except as described in sub-paragraph (ii).
   (ii) When it is impracticable to carry the all-round lights prescribed by Rule 27(b)(i) or Rule 28 below the masthead lights, they may be carried above the after masthead light(s) or vertically in between the forward masthead light(s) and the after masthead light(s) provided that in the latter case the requirement of Section 3(c) of this Annex shall be complied with.

> 2(f)(ii) discusses vessels restricted in ability to manoeuvre and constrained by draught.

(g) The sidelights of a power-driven vessel shall be placed at a height above the hull not greater than three-quarters of that of the forward masthead light. They shall not be so low as to be interfered with by deck lights.

> 2(g) discusses sidelight placement on PDVs.

(h) The sidelights, if in a combined lantern and carried on a power-driven vessel of less than 20m in length, shall be placed not less than 1m below the masthead light.

> 2(h) covers bicolour lights in relation to a masthead light.

ANNEX I – POSITIONING AND TECHNICAL DETAILS OF LIGHTS AND SHAPES

(i) When the Rules prescribe two or three lights to be carried in a vertical line, they shall be spaced as follows:
  (i) on a vessel of 20m in length or more such lights shall be spaced not less than 2m apart, and the lowest of these lights shall, except where a towing light is required, be placed at a height of not less than 4m above the hull;
  (ii) on a vessel of less than 20m in length such lights shall be spaced not less than 1m apart and the lowest of these lights shall, except where a towing light is required, be placed at a height of not less than 2m above the gunwale;
  (iii) when three lights are carried they shall be equally spaced.

> 2(i) discusses the spacing of CDB and RAM, NUC lights.

(j) The lower of the two all-round lights prescribed for a vessel when engaged in fishing shall be at a height above the sidelights not less than twice the distance between the two vertical lights.

> 2(j) discusses fishing vessel lights.

(k) The forward anchor light prescribed in Rule 30(a)(i), when two are carried, shall not be less than 4.5m above the after one. On a vessel of 50m or more in length this forward anchor light shall be placed at a height of not less than 6m above the hull.

> 2(k) discusses the positioning of anchor lights.

3. Horizontal positioning and spacing of lights

(a) When two masthead lights are prescribed for a power-driven vessel, the horizontal distance between them shall not be less than one-half of the length of the vessel but need not be more than 100m. The forward light shall be placed not more than one-quarter of the length of the vessel from the stem.

> 3(a) discusses masthead lights.

COLLISION REGULATIONS HANDBOOK

(b) On a power-driven vessel of 20m or more in length the sidelights shall not be placed in front of the forward masthead lights. They shall be placed at or near the side of the vessel.

> 3(b) discusses sidelights and their placement in relation to masthead lights.

(c) When the lights prescribed in Rule 27(b)(i) or Rule 28 are placed vertically between the forward masthead light(s) and the after masthead light(s) these all-round lights shall be placed at a horizontal distance of not less than 2m from the fore and aft centreline of the vessels in the athwartship direction.

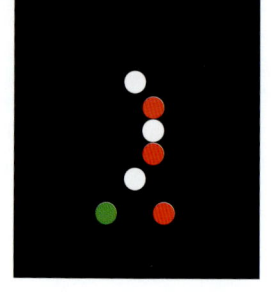

> 3(c) discusses vessels restricted in ability to manoeuvre and constrained by draught. Therefore, the RAM and CBD lights can be shifted off centre from the masthead lights.

(d) When only one masthead light is prescribed for a power-driven vessel, this light shall be exhibited forward of amidships; except that a vessel of less than 20m in length need not exhibit this light forward of amidships but shall exhibit it as far forward as is practicable.

> 3(d) discusses single masthead lights.

4. Details of location of direction-indicating lights for fishing vessels, dredgers and vessels engaged in underwater operations

(a) The light indicating the direction of the outlying gear from a vessel engaged in fishing as prescribed in Rule 26(c)(ii) shall be placed at a horizontal distance of not less than 2m and not more than 6m away from the two all-round red and white lights. This light shall be placed not higher than the all-round white light prescribed in Rule 26(c)(i) and not lower than the sidelights.

> 4(a) discussess the lights for outlying gear.

ANNEX I – POSITIONING AND TECHNICAL DETAILS OF LIGHTS AND SHAPES

(b) The lights and shapes on a vessel engaged in dredging or underwater operations to indicate the obstructed side and or the side on which it is safe to pass, as prescribed in Rule 27(d)(i) and (ii), shall be placed at the maximum practical horizontal distance, but in no case less than 2m, from the lights or shapes prescribed in Rule 27(b)(i) and (ii). In no case shall the upper of these lights or shapes be at a greater height than the lower of the three lights or shapes prescribed in Rule 27(b)(i) and (ii).

> 4(b) discusses dredging and underwater operations.

5. Screens for sidelights

The sidelights of vessels of 20m or more in length shall be fitted with inboard screens painted matt black, and meeting the requirements of Section 9 of this Annex. On vessels of less than 20m in length the sidelights, if necessary to meet the requirements of Section 9 of this Annex, shall be fitted with inboard matt black screens. With a combined lantern, using a single vertical filament and a very narrow division between the green and red sections, external screens need not be fitted.

6. Shapes

(a) Shapes shall be black and of the following sizes:
  (i) a ball shall have a diameter of not less than 0.6m;
  (ii) a cone shall have a base diameter of not less than 0.6m and a height equal to its diameter;
  (iii) a cylinder shall have a diameter of at least 0.6m and a height of twice its diameter;

> Therefore, a cylinder will be at least 0.6m by 1.2m high. Even then they will be difficult to see during the day.

  (iv) a diamond shape shall consist of two cones as defined in (ii) above having a common base.

> Therefore, the diamond shall be 1.2m in height.

COLLISION REGULATIONS HANDBOOK

(b) The vertical distance between shapes shall be at least 1.5m.

(c) In a vessel of less than 20m in length shapes of lesser dimensions but commensurate with the size of the vessel may be used and the distance apart may be correspondingly reduced.

> Small vessel anchor balls for use on vessels under 20m sold in chandleries are approximately 0.3m in diameter, but they should be 'commensurate with the size of the vessel'.

7. Colour specification of lights

The chromaticity of all navigation lights shall conform to the following standards, which lie within the boundaries of the area of the diagram specified for each colour by the International Commission on Illumination (CIE).

The boundaries of the area for each colour are given by indicating the corner co-ordinates, which are as follows:

(i)	White							
	x	0.525	0.525	0.452	0.310	0.310	0.443	
	y	0.382	0.440	0.440	0.348	0.283	0.382	
(ii)	Green							
	x	0.028	0.009	0.300	0.203			
	y	0.385	0.723	0.511	0.356			
(iii)	Red							
	x	0.680	0.660	0.735	0.721			
	y	0.320	0.320	0.265	0.259			
(iv)	Yellow							
	x	0.612	0.618	0.575	0.575			
	y	0.382	0.382	0.425	0.406			

ANNEX I – POSITIONING AND TECHNICAL DETAILS OF
LIGHTS AND SHAPES

8. Intensity of lights

(a) The minimum luminous intensity of lights shall be calculated by using

$$I = 3.43 \times 10^6 \times T \times D^2 \times K^{-D}$$

where:
- I is luminous intensity in candelas under service conditions,
- T is threshold factor 2×10^{-7} lux,
- D is range of visibility (luminous range) of the light in nautical miles,
- K is atmospheric transmissivity.

For prescribed lights the value of K shall be 0.8, corresponding to a meteorological visibility of approximately 13 nautical miles.

(b) A selection of figures derived from the formula is given in the following table:

Range of visibility (luminous range) of light in nautical miles D	Luminous intensity of light in candelas for K=0.8 I
1	0.9
2	4.3
3	12
4	27
5	52
6	94

Note: The maximum luminous intensity of navigation lights should be limited to avoid undue glare. This shall not be achieved by a variable control of the luminous intensity.

9. Horizontal sectors

(a)
  (i) In the forward direction, sidelights as fitted on the vessel shall show the minimum required intensities. The intensities shall decrease to reach practical cut-off between 1 degree and 3 degrees outside the prescribed sectors.

> This is so that there is no 'dark lane' for a very beamy vessel when viewed from right ahead.

(ii) For sternlights and masthead lights at 22.5 degrees abaft the beam for sidelights, the minimum required intensities shall be maintained over the arc of the horizon up to 5 degrees within the limits of the sectors prescribed in Rule 21. From 5 degrees within the prescribed sectors the intensity may decrease by 50 per cent up to the prescribed limits: it shall decrease steadily to reach practical cut-off at not more than 5 degrees outside the prescribed sectors.

> The consequence of this is that from 107.5 degrees to 117.5 degrees (relative) it may be possible to see all three lights (albeit somewhat faintly) and could give rise to doubt as to whether an overtaking situation exists.

(b)
   (i) All-round lights shall be so located as not to be obscured by masts, topmasts or structures within angular sectors of more than 6 degrees, except anchor lights prescribed in Rule 30, which need not be placed at an impracticable height above the hull.
   > Therefore a very small blind arc is allowed but should not exceed 6 degrees.
   (ii) If it is impracticable to comply with paragraph (b)(i) of this section by exhibiting only one all-round light, two all-round lights shall be used suitably positioned or screened so that they appear, as far as practicable, as one light at a distance of one mile.

10. Vertical sectors

(a) The vertical sectors of electric lights as fitted, with the exception of lights on sailing vessels underway shall ensure that:
   (i) at least the required minimum intensity is maintained at all angles from 5 degrees above to 5 degrees below the horizontal;
   (ii) at least 60 per cent of the required minimum intensity is maintained from 7.5 degrees above to 7.5 degrees below the horizontal.

> It should be noted, that if the luminous intensity drops, so does the visible range. At just 7.5 degrees it may reduce the luminosity and therefore the range by 40 per cent.

ANNEX I – POSITIONING AND TECHNICAL DETAILS OF LIGHTS AND SHAPES

(b) In the case of sailing vessels underway the vertical sectors of electric lights as fitted shall ensure that:
   (i) at least the required minimum intensity is maintained at all angles from 5 degrees above to 5 degrees below the horizontal;
   (ii) at least 50 per cent of the required minimum intensity is maintained from 25 degrees above to 25 degrees below the horizontal.

> A 20m sailing yacht (sidelights and sternlight intensity 2 miles), when well-heeled over, may be down to 1 mile visible range.

(c) In the case of lights other than electric these specifications shall be met as closely as possible.

11. Intensity of non-electric lights

Non-electric lights shall so far as practicable comply with the minimum intensities, as specified in the table given in Section 8 of this Annex.

> Modern low power consumption LED lights have all but removed any requirement for oil-burning navigation lights and anchor lights. However, there are a few still around often in far-flung places or small vessels of historic design.

12. Manoeuvring light

Notwithstanding the provisions of paragraph 2(f) of this Annex the manoeuvring light described in Rule 34(b) shall be placed in the same fore and aft vertical plane as the masthead light or lights and, where practicable, at a minimum height of 2m vertically above the forward masthead light, provided that it shall be carried not less than 2m vertically above or below the after masthead light. On a vessel where only one masthead light is carried the manoeuvring light, if fitted, shall be carried where it can best be seen, not less than 2m vertically apart from the masthead light.

> This clause states 'if fitted'. Rule 34(b) states that 'any vessel may supplement the whistle signal etc'. Therefore, we have a 'may' and an 'if fitted', meaning that this light, although useful, might not be considered a compulsory fit but would be highly useful at night to signal your intentions.

13. High-Speed Craft*

(a) The masthead light of high-speed craft may be placed at a height related to the breadth of the lower than that prescribed in paragraph 2(a)(i) of this Annex, provided that the base angle of the isosceles triangles formed by the sidelights and masthead light, when seen in end elevation, is not less than 27 degrees.

(b) On high-speed craft of 50m or more in length, the vertical separation between foremast and mainmast light of 4.5m required by paragraph 2(a)(ii) of this Annex may be modified provided that such distance shall not be less than the value determined by the following formula:

$$Y = \frac{(a + 17\Psi)C}{1000} + 2$$

where: Y is the height of the mainmast light above the foremast light in metres;

a is the height of the foremast light above the water surface in service condition in metres;

Ψ is the trim in service condition in degrees;

C is the horizontal separation of masthead lights in metres.

*Refer to the International Code of Safety for High-Speed Craft, 1994, and the International Code of Safety for High-Speed Craft, 2000.

14. Approval

The construction of lights and shapes and the installation of lights on board the vessel shall be to the satisfaction of the appropriate authority of the State whose flag the vessel is entitled to fly.

ANNEX II

Additional signals for fishing vessels fishing in close proximity

1. General

The lights mentioned herein shall, if exhibited in pursuance of Rule 26(d), be placed where they can best be seen. They shall be at least 0.9m apart but at a lower level than lights prescribed in Rule 26(b)(i) and (c)(i). The lights shall be visible all round the horizon at a distance of at least 1 mile but at a lesser distance than the lights prescribed by these Rules for fishing vessels.

> The additional lights are positioned below the green over white 26(b)(i) and red over white 26(c)(i).

2. Signals for trawlers

(a) Vessels of 20m or more in length when engaged in trawling, whether using demersal or pelagic gear, shall exhibit:
   (i) when shooting their nets, two white lights in a vertical line;
   (ii) when hauling their nets, one white light over one red light in a vertical line;
   (iii) when the net has come fast upon an obstruction, two red lights in a vertical line.

(b) Each vessel of 20m or more in length engaged in pair trawling shall exhibit:
   (i) by night, a searchlight directed forward and in the direction of the other vessel of the pair;
   (ii) when shooting or hauling their nets or when the nets have come fast upon an obstruction, the lights prescribed in 2(a) above.
   (iii) A vessel of less than 20m in length engaged in trawling, whether using

COLLISION REGULATIONS HANDBOOK

demersal or pelagic gear or engaged in pair trawling, may exhibit the lights prescribed in paragraphs (a) or (b) of this Section, as appropriate.

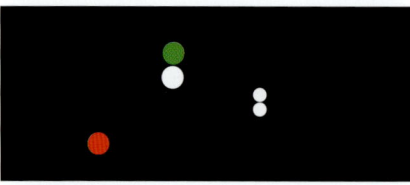

- Vessel engaged in trawling, underway and making way
- Port aspect
- Less than 50m
- Shooting nets

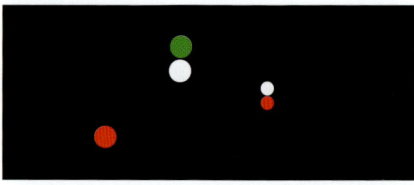

- Vessel engaged in trawling, underway and making way
- Port aspect
- Less than 50m
- Hauling nets

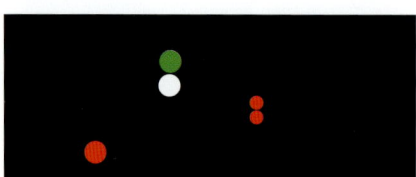

- Vessel engaged in trawling
- Port aspect
- Less than 50m
- Nets fast

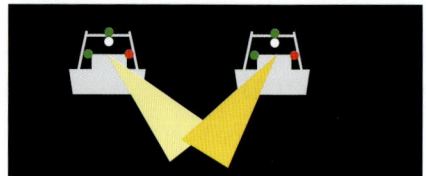

- Pair trawling

While the rules state that vessels over 20m shall show the additional lights, (b)(iii) states that vessels under 20 metres may exhibit the lights. Size (+/- 20m) cannot really be deduced from these additional lights.

3. Signals for purse seiners

Vessels engaged in fishing with purse seine gear may exhibit two yellow lights in a vertical line. These lights shall flash alternately every second and with equal light and occultation duration. These lights may be exhibited only when the vessel is hampered by its fishing gear.

Shown with red/white lights as the vessel is 'fishing rather than trawling'.

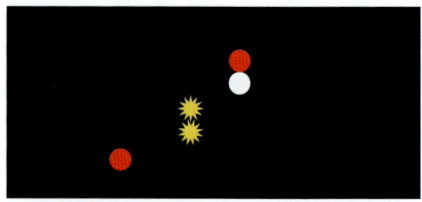

- Vessel engaged in fishing, underway and making way
- Purse seiner hampered by nets
- Port aspect
- Yellow lights are alternate and flashing
- Port aspect

114

ANNEX III

Technical details of sound signal appliances

1. Whistles

(a) Frequencies and range of audibility
The fundamental frequency of the signal shall lie within the range 70–700 Hz. The range of audibility of the signal from a whistle shall be determined by those frequencies, which may include the fundamental and/or one or more higher frequencies, which lie within the range 180–700 Hz (+/-1%) for a vessel of 20m or more in length, or 180–2100Hz (+/-1%) for a vessel of less than 20m in length and which provide the sound pressure levels specified in paragraph l(c) below.

(b) Limits of fundamental frequencies
To ensure a wide variety of whistle characteristics, the fundamental frequency of a whistle shall be between the following limits:
(i) 70–200 Hz, for a vessel 200m or more in length;
(ii) 130–350 Hz, for a vessel 75m but less than 200m in length;
(iii) 250–700 Hz, for a vessel less than 75m in length.

(c) Sound signal intensity and range of audibility
A whistle fitted in a vessel shall provide, in the direction of maximum intensity of the whistle and at a distance of 1m from it, a sound pressure level in at least one 1/3rd-octave band within the range of frequencies 180–700 Hz (+/-1%) for a vessel of 20m or more in length, or 180–2100 Hz (+/-1%) for a vessel of less than 20m in length, of not less than the appropriate figure given in the table below.

Length of vessel in m	1/3rd-octave band level at 1m in dB referred to 2x10⁻⁵N/m²	Audibility range in nautical miles
200 or more	143	2
75 but less than 200	138	1.5
20 but less than 75	130	1
Less than 20	120*	
	115 †	0.5
	111 ‡	

* When the measured frequencies lie within the range 180–450 Hz
† When the measured frequencies lie within the range 450–800 Hz
‡ When the measured frequencies lie within the range 800–2100 Hz

The range of audibility in the table above is for information and is approximately the range at which a whistle may be heard on its forward axis with 90 per cent probability in conditions of still air on board a vessel having average background noise level at the listening posts (taken to be 68 dB in the octave band centred on 250 Hz and 63 dB in the octave band centred on 500 Hz).

> The range is measured on its forward axis, therefore there is a large chance that the whistle's range is reduced on the vessel's beam and astern. (d) below indicates that the range in any direction will be at least half of that in the forward axis. Therefore, while the range may be 2 miles ahead, it may be just over a mile astern.

In practice the range at which a whistle may be heard is extremely variable and depends critically on weather conditions; the values given can be regarded as typical but under conditions of strong wind or high ambient noise level at the listening post the range may be much reduced.

(d) Directional properties

The sound pressure level of a directional whistle shall be not more than 4 dB below the prescribed sound pressure level on the axis at any direction in the horizontal plane within ±45 degrees of the axis. The sound pressure level at any other direction in the horizontal plane shall be not more than 10 dB below the prescribed sound pressure level on the axis, so that the range in any direction will be at least half the range on the

ANNEX III – TECHNICAL DETAILS OF SOUND SIGNAL APPLIANCES

forward axis. The sound pressure level shall be measured in that 1/3rd-octave band which determines the audibility range.

(e) Positioning of whistles
When a directional whistle is to be used as the only whistle on a vessel, it shall be installed with its maximum intensity directed straight ahead.

A whistle shall be placed as high as practicable on a vessel, in order to reduce interception of the emitted sound by obstructions and also to minimize hearing damage risk to personnel. The sound pressure level of the vessel's own signal at listening posts shall not exceed 110 dB (A) and so far as practicable should not exceed 100 dB (A).

> Noise is measured in decibels (dB). An 'A-weighting', sometimes written as dB (A), is used to measure average noise levels. Under Merchant Shipping Regulations, a risk assessment may be required to ensure that look-outs are not placed in positions that could damage hearing as they will be torn between protection of hearing using Personal Protective Equipment and keeping a look-out by sight, hearing, etc.

(f) Fitting of more than one whistle
If whistles are fitted at a distance apart of more than 100m, it shall be so arranged that they are not sounded simultaneously.

(g) Combined whistle systems
If due to the presence of obstructions the sound field of a single whistle or one of the whistles referred to in paragraph 1(f) above is likely to have a zone of greatly reduced signal level, it is recommended that a combined whistle system be fitted so as to overcome this reduction. For the purposes of the Rules a combined whistle system is to be regarded as a single whistle. The whistles of a combined system shall be located at a distance apart of not more than 100m and arranged to be sounded simultaneously. The frequency of any one whistle shall differ from those of the others by at least 10 Hz.

2. Bell or gong
(a) Intensity of signal
A bell or gong, or other device having similar sound characteristics shall produce a sound pressure level of not less than 110 dB at a distance of 1m from it.

(b) Construction
Bells and gongs shall be made of corrosion-resistant material and designed to give a clear tone. The diameter of the mouth of the bell shall be not less than 300mm

for vessels of 20m or more in length. Where practicable, a power-driven bell striker is recommended to ensure constant force but manual operation shall be possible. The mass of the striker shall be not less than 3 per cent of the mass of the bell.

3. Approval

The construction of sound signal appliances, their performance and their installation on board the vessel shall be to the satisfaction of the appropriate authority of the State whose flag the vessel is entitled to fly.

ANNEX IV

Distress signals

1. The following signals, used or exhibited either together or separately, indicate distress and need of assistance:

(a) a gun or other explosive signals fired at intervals of about a minute;
(b) a continuous sounding with any fog-signalling apparatus;
(c) rockets or shells, throwing red stars fired one at a time at short intervals;
(d) a signal made by any signalling method consisting of the group ... --- ... (SOS) in the Morse Code;
(e) a signal sent by radiotelephony consisting of the spoken word MAYDAY;
(f) the International Code Signal of distress indicated by N.C.;
(g) a signal consisting of a square flag having above or below it a ball or anything resembling a ball;
(h) flames on the vessel (as from a burning tar barrel, oil barrel, etc.);
(i) a rocket parachute flare or a hand-flare showing a red light;
(j) a smoke signal giving off orange-coloured smoke;
(k) slowly and repeatedly raising and lowering arms outstretched to each side;
(l) a distress alert by means of digital selective calling (DSC) transmitted on:
    (i) VHF channel 70; or
    (ii) MF/HF on the frequencies 2187.5 kHz, 8414.5 kHz, 4207.5 kHz, 6312 kHz, 12577 kHz or 16804.5 kHz;
(m) a ship-to-shore distress alert transmitted by the ship's Inmarsat or other mobile satellite service provider ship earth station;
(n) signals transmitted by emergency position-indicating radio beacons;
(o) approved signals transmitted by radiocommunications systems, including survival craft radar transponders.

COLLISION REGULATIONS HANDBOOK

The spoken word "MAYDAY" sent by radiotelephony	Radiotelegraph alarm signal DSC	Radiotelegraph alarm signal DSC	Morse SOS by radio or any other signalling method
Gun or noise at 1 minute intervals	Continuous sound with fog signal	Red parachute or hand flares	Rockets or shells throwing red stars at short intervals
Flames or smoke	Orange smoke	Code flags 'N' and 'C'	A square shape above or below a ball shape
SART Radar transponder	**EPIRB** Emergency position indicating radio beacon	Outstretched arms waved slowly up and down	Dye marker

2. The use or exhibition of any of the foregoing signals, except for the purpose of indicating distress and need of assistance and the use of other signals which may be confused with any of the above signals, is prohibited.

3. Attention is drawn to the relevant sections of the International Code of Signals, the International Aeronautical and Maritime Search and Rescue Manual, Volume III, and the following signals:
(a) a piece of orange-coloured canvas with either a black square and circle or other appropriate symbol (for identification from the air);
(b) a dye marker.

Extract from IMO Resolution A.1004(25) – Adoption Of Amendments to the International Regulations For Preventing Collisions at Sea, 1972. (Adopted On 29 November 2007)

WATCHKEEPING

The collision regulations are not supposed to be a stand-alone document. They work alongside regulations laid down in the STCW Code Chapter VIII (watchkeeping), guidance given in MCA M Notice MGN 315 and the ICS Bridge Procedures Guide. Together they link ColRegs and bridge watchkeeping regulations so that they work harmoniously.

To amplify this and really understand COLREGS Section 1, Rule 5 (look-out), MGN 315 and STCW Chapter VIII all give guidance on responsibilities of a look-out and considerations for increasing a look-out. It will also be noted that there are similarities between Rule 6 (Safe speed) and the acceptance of a sole look-out (or not). There is also official guidance on how the Master is required to organize the watch and when the Master would be called out of their bunk.

Therefore this section on watchkeeping is fundamental to how the ColRegs are applied at sea and how those Masters, OOWs and crew go about complying with their ColRegs' responsibilities (Rule 2).

Responsibilities

Onboard a vessel that is operating watches, the make-up of the vessel's crew could be a Master and a single mate, or a full complement of bridge watch officers making up the team, or the vessel may have a single manning exemption and be restricted to short voyages and other requirements.

No matter how many seafarers the safe manning document or regulations require for the type of vessel, all watchkeeping will follow the same principles of safe navigation and collision avoidance.

Master

The Master must ensure that watchkeeping arrangements are adequate for maintaining a safe navigational or cargo watch. Under the Master's general direction, the officers/crew of the navigational watch are responsible for navigating the ship safely during their periods of duty, when they will be particularly concerned with avoiding collision and stranding.

Officer of the Watch (OOW)

The nominated Officer of the Watch (OOW) or Watchkeeper is the Master's representative and is primarily responsible at all times for the safe navigation of the ship and for complying with the ColRegs. The lead OOW may oversee other officers on the bridge, depending on the vessel size and make-up.

Chief Engineer

The Chief Engineer, in consultation with the Master, is to ensure that watchkeeping arrangements are adequate to maintain a safe engineering watch.

Look-outs

Depending on the size of vessel, type of operation and visibility, extra look-outs may be required to report back to the OOW or Master.

Watch arrangements and duties

Whether the vessel has a complement of officers or just a Master and Mate, the same formula is used to take account of who is involved in watchkeeping duties.

	Considerations when deciding who forms part of the watch and how it is organised
1	Appropriately qualified and experienced personnel
2	At no time shall the bridge be left unattended
3	Traffic density
4	Weather conditions, visibility and daylight or darkness
5	Proximity of navigational hazards
6	Use and operational condition of navigational aids
7	Whether the ship is fitted with automatic steering
8	Whether there are radio duties to be performed
9	Unmanned machinery space controls, alarms/indicators on the bridge
10	Any demands on the watch due to special operational circumstances

Taking or handing over the watch

The watch should not be handed over if the relief is not capable of carrying out the watch effectively. In this event, notify the Master.

Both the relieved and relieving officer shall ensure that the relieving watch are

WATCHKEEPING

capable of performing their duties and ensure their vision is fully adjusted to the light conditions before taking over the watch.

The OOW shall give watchkeeping personnel all appropriate instructions and information to ensure the keeping of a safe watch, including look-out.

Current status

Prior to taking over the watch, the OOW should satisfy themselves as to the ship's position and confirm her intended track, course and speed and note any expected dangers to navigation during their watch.

Obligations

	Obligations. A relieving watch should satisfy themselves on the:
1	Masters standing orders with reference to safe navigation
2	Position, course, speed and draught of the ship
3	Effect of tides, currents, weather and visibility upon course and speed
4	Procedures for the use of main engines to manoeuvre
5	Navigational situation, including, but not limited to:
5.1	operational condition/limitations of all bridge and safety equipment
5.2	errors of compasses
5.3	presence and movement of ships in the vicinity
5.4	conditions and hazards likely to be encountered
5.5	effects of heel, trim, water density, squat on under-keel clearance

If the OOW is to be relieved when a manoeuvre or action to avoid any hazard is taking place, the relief shall be deferred until the action is completed.

Look-out

For compliance with the ColRegs, a proper look-out shall be maintained at all times and shall serve the purpose of:

Look-out's responsibilities	
1	Maintaining a continuous state of vigilance by sight and hearing, as well as by all other available means
2	Fully appraising the situation and the risk of collision, stranding and other dangers to navigation
3	Detecting ships or aircraft in distress, shipwrecked persons, wrecks, debris and other hazards to safe navigation

The look-out must give their full attention to keeping a proper look-out and not be assigned or undertake anything that could interfere with that task.

The duties of the look-out and helmsperson are separate. A helmsperson shall not be considered to be the look-out while steering, except in small ships where an unobstructed all-round view is provided at the steering position.

To ensure an adequate look-out is maintained, the Master should consider the following:

Considerations for adequate look-out	
1	Visibility, state of weather and sea
2	Traffic density
3	Required attention when near traffic separation schemes (TSS) or busy channels
4	Additional workload caused by the ship's functions, operating requirements and manoeuvres
5	Crew member fitness for duty – on call or assigned to the watch
6	Knowledge and confidence in officers and crew competence
7	Officer experience and familiarity with ship equipment, procedures & manoeuvring
8	Availability of bridge assistance to be summoned when necessary
9	The operational status of instrumentation, controls and alarms
10	The size of vessel and field of vision available
11	Bridge layout, which might inhibit detection of external developments

WATCHKEEPING

Sole look-out

The STCW code states that the OOW may be the sole look-out in daylight provided that, on each occasion:

1. The situation has been carefully assessed and it has been established without doubt that it is safe to do so.

2. Full account has been taken of:

    - state of weather;
    - visibility;
    - traffic density;
    - proximity of dangers to navigation and the attention necessary when in or near TSS.

3. Assistance is immediately available to be summoned when required.

> The MCA considers it dangerous and irresponsible for the OOW to act as sole look-out during periods of darkness or restricted visibility.

Performing the navigational watch

The officer of the navigational watch shall keep the watch on the bridge and in no circumstances leave the bridge until properly relieved.

They continue to be responsible for the safe navigation of the vessel despite the presence of the Master on the bridge until informed specifically that the Master has assumed the 'con' and this is mutually understood. If the bridge is operated solely by the Master, the following good practice is still applicable.

	Good bridge practice requires the nominated OOW to:
1	Notify the Master when in any doubt as to what action to take in the interests of safety
2	Understand that the perceptions of other vessels' watch officers may differ from your perception
3	Keep a proper navigation record during the watch
4	Ensure the vessel is steered manually when any potentially hazardous situation needs to be dealt with or in areas of high traffic density and restricted visibility
5	Use the radar at all times in areas of high traffic density and whenever restricted visibility is encountered or expected
6	Frequently check the vessel's position, course and speed using all appropriate navigational aids to ensure that the vessel follows the planned track
7	Take frequent fixes by more than one method
8	Use the largest scale chart on board, suitable for the area and corrected with the latest available information

Distractions

When on the bridge do not undertake any other duties that would interfere or compromise the keeping of a safe navigational watch. Therefore, do not catch up on paperwork, chart corrections and auditing the vessel's SMS.

Ensure there are no distractions caused by the use of domestic radios, audio players, personal computers, TVs, mobile phones, tablets, etc.

Pilot

The Master or OOW (if the Master is off the bridge) is responsible for the vessel despite a pilot being on board.

If in any doubt as to the pilot's actions or intentions, seek clarification from the pilot;

if doubt still exists, notify the Master and take whatever action is necessary until the Master arrives.

Notifying the Master

The Master will write particular standing orders and these will include times when it is mandatory to call the Master.

	Notifying the Master. The OOW shall notify the Master immediately:
1	If restricted visibility is encountered or expected
2	If the traffic conditions or the movements of other ships are causing concern
3	If difficulty is experienced in maintaining course
4	Failure to sight land, navigation mark or sounding by the expected time
5	Unexpectedly sighting land, navigation mark or sounding
6	Breakdown of: engines, steering, navigational equipment, alarm or indicator
7	If the radio equipment malfunctions
8	In heavy weather, if in any doubt about the possibility of weather damage
9	If the ship meets any hazard to navigation, such as ice or a derelict
10	In any other emergency or if in any doubt

The officer in charge of the navigational watch shall, in addition to notifying the Master, not hesitate to take immediate action for the safety of the ship, where circumstances require.

EXAM PREPARATION

While it is important, and your legal responsibility, to know the Collision Regulations, occasionally we are examined by a Flag State or an authority for an exam and it is useful to be prepared.

Knowing the rules

It is not normal to need to know the rules by their number, part or section. However, if you are revising for an OOW, Mate or Masters exam, the amount of time you will put into studying the rules will probably mean that you will become quite familiar with many of the numbers and it is probable that many studying will end up knowing Rules 5–19 by number.

If you try to show off and state the number each time, the examiner may catch you off guard and ask you what Rule 28 or 36 is and while we may know our lights and signals well, we may not know the rule numbers for them and it may catch you unawares.

However, knowing the following will help:

PART A GENERAL RULES (1–3)
Rules 1–3 include application, responsibilities and definitions and therefore always apply.
Part B STEERING AND SAILING RULES
Section I – Conduct of vessels in any conditions of visibility (4–10)
These rules apply at all times. It could be said that as they contain look-out, safe speed, risk of collision and actions to avoid, this forms part of how you would organize and run your bridge and vessel.
Section II – Conduct of vessels in sight of one another (11–18)
This section of rules only applies when in sight of the other vessel. It would always be used with the rules in Section I but not normally in conjunction with Section III.
Section III – Conduct of vessels in restricted visibility (19)
This section would normally only be used with the rules in Section I.

Letting examiners know you know the rules

What you do need to do is to know the rules and then know how to apply them. This means knowing what the other vessel is telling you by their course, state, aspect, light or signal and then knowing what they and you would do in that circumstance.

It is a common mistake for people to memorize the words of the rules but not put the time in to be able to apply them correctly or think about what the rules actually are requiring vessels to do – so, therefore, concentrate on the application as this is often where you will get caught out. For instance, when looking at a vessel's lights, we need

EXAM PREPARATION

to know what type of vessel, size, aspect, etc., but then also what we would do about it and how we would act when seeing it. Furthermore, how we would act if the other vessel does not take the action it is supposed to.

A useful way to let examiners know that you know the rules is to be able to apply them correctly. Also use some of the terminology and wording from the rules in your answers.

A useful strategy when answering is remembering D.O.A. as this can break down the rule for you and give you time to think.

D.O.A

Determine
Determine whether a risk of collision exists by taking a series of bearings and establishing whether the bearings are constant (or near constant). (Rule 7)

Obligation
- What is our obligation? Is it in sight or restricted visibility?
- Are we stand-on, give-way; or is it an impeding situation?
- Is it head-on, crossing, overtaking or forward/aft of the beam in restricted visibility?

Act
- What are our actions?
- Will we keep clear – slow down, turn to port, turn to starboard, stand-on or stand-on with caution?
- When doing so, shall we indicate our manoeuvre by sound/light and how will we act?

Rule 8 (actions to avoid collision) casts light on useful terms that we can use to explain our answers and actions.

Considerations when taking action
- Positive
- Made in ample time
- With due regard to the observance of good seamanship
- Does not result in another close-quarters situation.

How much to act
- Positive
- Substantial

129

- Large enough to be readily apparent to another vessel observing visually or by radar
- A succession of small alterations of course and/or speed should be avoided.

Result of action
- Passing at a safe distance.
- Effectiveness of the action shall be carefully checked until the other vessel is finally past and clear.
- Does not result in another close-quarters situation.

Still unsure?
A vessel shall slacken her speed or take all way off by stopping or reversing her means of propulsion.

Other problem areas

Lights
- Know the difference in lights between underway and making way.
- Know the difference between vessels aground and at anchor.
- Look at the small differences between RAM and fishing vessels at anchor.

Sounds
- Know the difference between sounds when in sight of another vessel and sounds used in restricted visibility. Rule 34(a) states that 'when in sight of one another' a power-driven vessel underway shall indicate her manoeuvre to take action by use of the signal whistle.
- Review the repetition intervals in restricted visibility between vessels underway and those at anchor and aground.

RADAR AND PLOTTING BASICS

Collisions have frequently been caused by failure to make proper use of radar and radar plotting aids in both restricted visibility and clear weather. Common errors are deciding to alter course on the basis of insufficient (scanty) information, not using long-range scanning to see what is ahead and maintaining too high a speed, particularly when a close-quarters situation is developing.

Information provided by radar and radar plotting aids in clear weather conditions can assist the watchkeeper in maintaining a proper look-out in areas of high traffic density. It is most important to remember that navigation in restricted visibility can be more demanding and great care is needed even with all the information available from the radar and radar plotting aids.

Where continuous radar watchkeeping and plotting cannot be maintained, even greater caution must be exercised. A 'safe speed' should at all times reflect the prevailing circumstances.

SOLAS regulations on radar plotting aids

Radars must be equipped with plotting aids, the type of which is dependent upon the size of ship as follows:

Watchkeepers must be fully conversant with the operation and limitations of these plotting facilities and should practise using them in clear weather conditions to improve their skills.

Type	Performance	Vessel type (SOLAS Ch.V R19)
Electronic Plotting Aid (EPA)	EPA equipment enables electronic plotting of at least 10 targets, but without automatic acquisition or tracking	Ships between 300 and 500 gross tonnage (GT)
Automatic Tracking Aid (ATA)	ATA equipment enables manual acquisition and automatic tracking and display of at least 10 targets	On ships of 500 GT and upwards
Automatic Tracking Aid (ATA)	ATA equipment enables manual acquisition and automatic tracking and display of at least 10 targets	On ships of 3,000 GT and over the second radar must also be equipped with an ATA, the two ATAs must be functionally independent of each other.
Automatic Radar Plotting Aid (ARPA)	ARPA provides for manual or automatic acquisition of targets and the automatic tracking and display of all relevant target information for at least 20 targets for anti-collision decision making. It also enables trial manoeuvre to be executed	Ships of 10,000 GT and over

Smaller vessels that do not fall under the SOLAS requirements above may have radar fitted that uses a Mini Automatic Radar Plotting Aid (MARPA) or an Electronic Bearing Line (EBL), variable range marker (VRM), pencil and paper.

Some small commercial vessels do not have radar fitted mandatorily but can do so. Many leisure vessels do not have radar.

It is a requirement under SOLAS that vessels under 150 GT fit a radar reflector, if practicable. Therefore, an interpretation of this could be that a small inflatable boat might not fit a radar reflector, but if it had an arch it would.

Establishing a risk of collision using radar

To establish whether a risk of collision exists, the technique of checking for a constant bearing is used, just like when in sight of another vessel, but this time we can also calculate range and bearing using radar.

This calculation can be done manually by systematic plotting on a sheet, or automatically if the radar has MARPA/ARPA.

There are three ways to establish whether a risk of collision exists when using radar:
1. Use the electronic bearing line (EBL) to identify contacts on a constant bearing.
2. Manual systematic plotting of those contacts until the danger is clear.

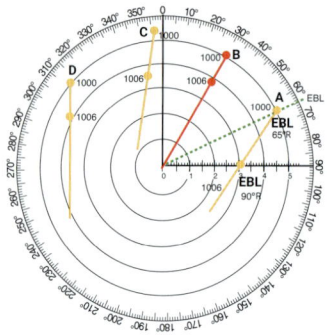

▲ Note: Third prediction plots removed for clarity

3. Automatic systematic plotting using ARPA – MARPA – ATA to acquire a vessel and automatically plot the contact.

Using the EBL

The EBL originates from the centre of the screen, which is our position. The EBL is pointed at any contact on screen and any contact that stays on or close to that line (constant bearing) indicates a high collision risk. If there are multiple targets they can be marked with a pen (on a transparency overlaying the screen), and their positions compared after an interval of time; prediction can also be made of how they will continue to move relative to our heading.

Above, we have four targets and at 1000 we note their position and range by placing the EBL on them one at a time. Our vessel is travelling at 10 knots, travelling 000° (N).
- Contact A. Using the EBL, at 1000 the bearing of contact was 065°. Six minutes later, the bearing had changed to 090°. There is no risk of collision.

RADAR AND PLOTTING BASICS

- Contact B. The bearing is steady on the EBL and range has decreased – therefore a collision will occur without avoidance action.
- Contact C. The bearing is changing between 1000 and 1006. By extending a line through the two contacts, we can see that the vessel will pass about one mile away on our port side, if she stays on course.
- Contact D. The bearing of the contact has changed significantly so the vessel should pass clear.
- The 1000 and 1006 position is parallel to our course, but in the opposite direction, indicating Target D is a stationary object.

MGN 379 (Navigation: use of electronic navigation aids) states: 'The compass bearing, either visual or radar, should be used to assess risk of collision. The relative bearing of a target should not be used when own ship's course and/or speed alters, as risk of collision may still exist, even where the relative bearing is changing. Mariners should also be aware that at close range, risk of collision may exist even with a changing compass bearing.'

Plotting interval

The plotting interval is usually 6 minutes (1/10th of an hour) because it makes our sums easier. For instance, at 10 knots, in 6 minutes we will travel 1 mile (1/10th of 10 knots = 1nm in 6 minutes). After 6 minutes the EBL is placed over the contact again to establish their relative track over that time, or whether they are staying on the same bearing.

Manual radar plotting

To gain more information from the contact we can manually record the contacts on a plotting sheet at regular intervals. Realistically, this is not done on vessels anymore, but is a regular occurrence in examinations to check understanding. Plotting sheets are often A4 size and allow radar contacts to be monitored. The rings on the plotting sheet and the horizontal scale line allow easy transferral between what is on the radar screen and what you plot on the sheet.

Terms

		A	Another
		WO	Way of Own (vessel over the time period)
CPA	Closest Point of Approach		
TCPA	Time to Closest Point of Approach	WA	Way of Another (vessel over that time period)
W	Way		
O	Observed (this is the observed object)	OA	Observed Actual relative direction of another gives the Closest Point of Approach

Examples

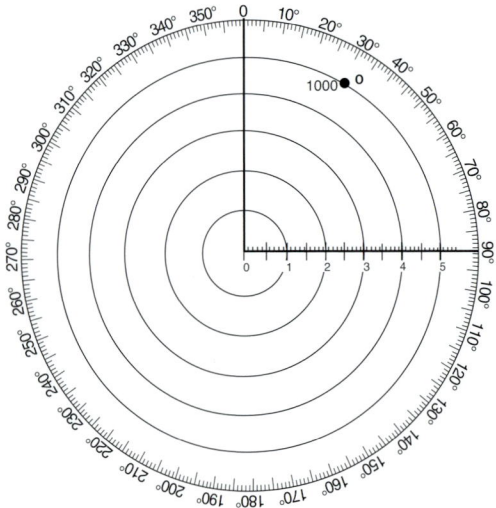

In all the examples our own vessel's speed is 10 knots and the course 020° when a contact comes into view.

Note on the radar plotting sheet your vessels details such as:
- Ship's speed
- Head up, Course up or North up
- Range and range rings in use.

Mark the bearing of the first radar contact, the range and time.

Contact ID			1	
Time		Range		Bearing
1st	1000	5nm		032°
2nd		nm		°
3rd		nm		°
CPA	nm	TCPA		
Speed (WA)		Knt		
Heading	° R	Heading		°T

RADAR AND PLOTTING BASICS

This contact is labelled O (Observed).

Contact ID		1	
Time		Range	Bearing
1st	1000	5nm	032°
2nd	1006	4nm	029°
3rd	1012	3nm	025°
CPA	0.8nm	TCPA	1030
Speed (WA)		Knt	
Heading	° R	Heading	°T

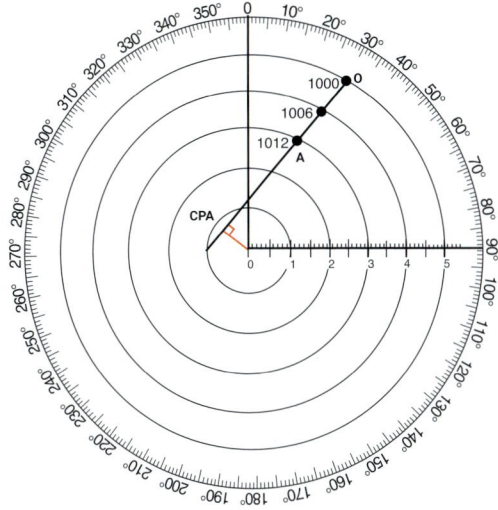

Every six minutes note and plot the bearings and record the time. After the second 6-minute interval (1012) draw a line through the O and A contacts, then continue the line to establish if there is a risk of collision.

Using more 6-minute plots averages out inconsistencies in the contact bearings.

By extending this line down towards the centre, it gives the approaching contacts' CPA, which is measured at right angles. In this case, the CPA is approximately 0.8nm.

COLLISION REGULATIONS HANDBOOK

To establish the time to CPA (TCPA), measure the distance the echo travelled in 6 or 12 minutes along OA, and then project it forwards in 6- or 12-minute increments to the point of CPA. In this case, TCPA would be about 1030.

Contact ID		1	
Time		Range	Bearing
1st	1000	5nm	032°
2nd	1006	4nm	029°
3rd	1012	3nm	025°
CPA	0.8nm	TCPA	1030
Speed (WA)		Knt	
Heading	° R	Heading	°T

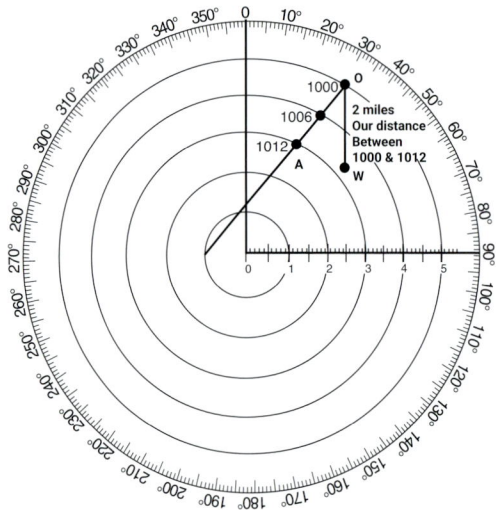

RADAR AND PLOTTING BASICS

To gain more information about the contact, such as aspect and speed, we plot our vessel's movement over the same period. At 10 knots, our vessel has travelled 2 miles in 12 minutes. From the initial contact, two miles are marked off from (O) in the opposite direction, and parallel to our heading marker. The end of this line is marked W (Way). The line WO represents the 'Way of our Own' vessel.

Contact ID		1	
Time		Range	Bearing
1st	1000	5nm	032°
2nd	1006	4nm	029°
3rd	1012	3nm	025°
CPA	0.8nm	TCPA	1030
Speed (WA)		Knt	
Heading	° R	Heading	°T

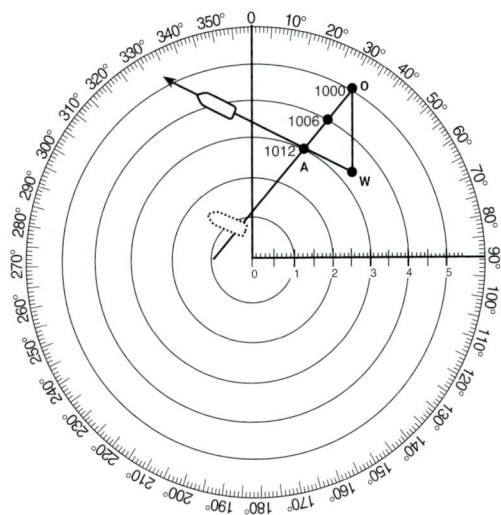

COLLISION REGULATIONS HANDBOOK

What we know so far is that an object is closing and will pass across our bow with a CPA of 0.8nm. We do not know the aspect and whether it is the port bow or the port quarter that will be seen. Our next line gives us this information.

Label the 1012 contact A (Another). Draw a line from W through the 1012 contact to create WA (Way of Another). This is an indication of the actual aspect of the approaching contact. Therefore, when it actually reaches the point of CPA a sternlight would be seen.

Contact ID		1	
Time		Range	Bearing
1st	1000	5nm	032°
2nd	1006	4nm	029°
3rd	1012	3nm	025°
CPA	0.8nm	TCPA	1030
Speed (WA)		Knt 1.3/2=6.5 knt	
Heading	292° R	Heading	312°T

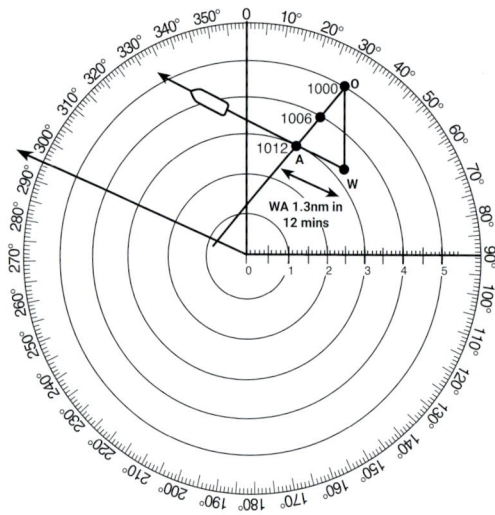

Extra information is available about the vessel such as her speed and her actual heading. To obtain speed, measure the WA line. Remember that it is based over 12 minutes (2/10ths of an hour). In the example, WA is 1.3nm over 12 minutes, therefore it would have travelled half that distance, 0.65nm, in 6 minutes (1/10th of an hour): 0.65 x 10 = 6.5. Therefore, the vessel is travelling at 6.5 knots.

RADAR AND PLOTTING BASICS

The contact's relative course is determined by transferring the WA line to the centre of the plotting sheet so that a bearing can be read, in this instance 292°R (Relative course).

The contact's True course can be obtained if our vessel's heading of 020° is taken into account.

292°R + 020°Hdg = Contact 312°T at 6.5 knots

Contact ID		1	
Time		Range	Bearing
1st	1000	5nm	032°
2nd	1006	4nm	029°
3rd	1012	3nm	025°
CPA	0.8nm	TCPA	1030
Speed (WA)		Knt 1.3/2=6.5 knt	
Heading	292° R	Heading	312°T

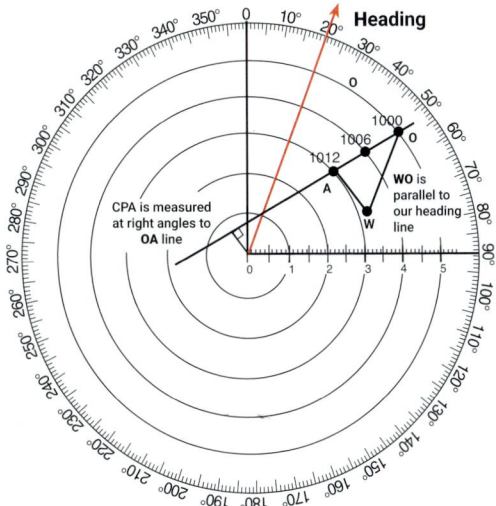

If the radar is in North up, then our vessel's heading line is plotted first. The contacts are then plotted in exactly the same way. Using the same example, the bearings are no longer Relative, they would be True bearings and therefore be 20° different. WO is plotted reciprocal to our course (020° = 200°) and the plot constructed in a similar way.

The only difference is that the heading of the contact requires no further adjustment from Relative to True.

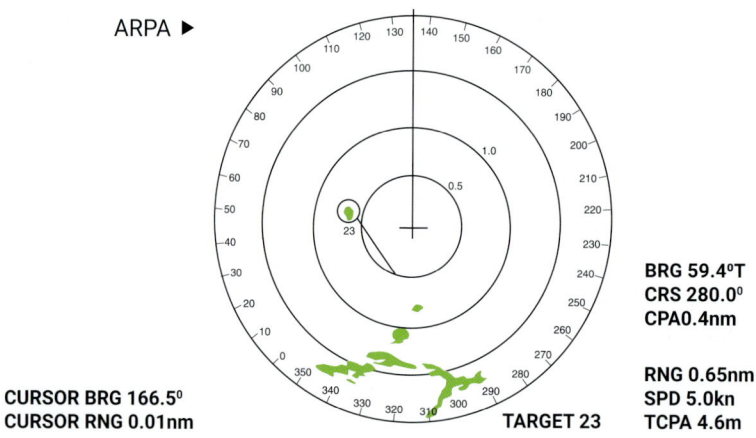

ARPA and MARPA

ARPA/MARPA automatically plots the contacts once they have been acquired and outputs the data such as CPA and TCPA on screen. An alarm sounds if a contact's projected CPA comes under a user-defined limit.

ARPA and MARPA require electronic data inputs of:
- heading via an electronic compass
- speed, via a GPS or speed log.

With this information, as was done manually before, the contact's data is automatically calculated and displayed on screen.

Because this radar is doing the calculation it will give the results very quickly, usually after ten seconds, but the data will require vigilance as it will change once the plot has settled down over time.

TARGET 23	
BRG 59.4°T	RNG 0.65nm
CRS 280.0°	SPD 5.0kn
CPA 0.4nm	TCPA 4.6m

A type-approved ARPA should provide the following data of the other target in specified time frames with 95 per cent probability values:

Within one minute:
- Relative course
- Relative speed
- CPA (Closest Point of Approach).

Within three minutes:
- Relative course
- Relative speed
- CPA (Closest Point of Approach)
- TCPA (Time to Closest Point of Approach)
- True course
- True speed.

RADAR AND PLOTTING BASICS

If an automatic plotting aid is used, ensure speed and heading inputs are satisfactory. Serious errors can arise if heading and/or speed inputs are incorrect or the speed of data transfer is too slow; e.g. an electronic compass that is too slow to input data results in ARPA images jumping about the screen and ARPA data that is useless. Heading inputs would be from a gyro, a satellite compass or a suitable transmitting magnetic heading device (TMHD).

If two radars are fitted it is good practice, especially in restricted visibility or in congested waters, for one to be designated for anti-collision work, while the other is used to assist navigation or on different ranges to assist in long-range scanning. If only one of the radars is fitted with ARPA then this should be the one used for anti-collision work and the other for navigation.

Masters and watchkeepers must be fully conversant with the operation and limitations of these plotting facilities and should practise using them in clear weather conditions to improve their skills. These aids will only work if the set is adjusted correctly so that contacts are seen and that the range is changed to see the overall picture.

Sea and ground stabilisation

If a small vessel 'stand-alone radar' is not linked to any other piece of equipment apart from its own scanner, it allows a 'Head up' display to be used only.

When radar is linked to heading information, it is said to be a basic 'stabilised radar' and will also allow a 'North up' view.

When radar is linked to speed and heading information it is 'stabilised radar' and can further be defined as either a sea or ground stabilised radar:

- 'Sea stabilised' uses inputs for heading from an on-board magnetic or gyro heading sensor and speed from an in-water transducer log (Doppler or paddlewheel). The compass should give a fast rate of data to provide good information.
- 'Ground stabilised' uses GPS COG (course over the ground) or a heading sensor and GPS SOG (speed over the ground) to provide calculations based on the vessel's relationship and position to the earth.

Collision avoidance should use 'Sea stabilisation' because our vessel and the contact are moving on the same body of water and could be affected by tide and leeway. Note: Many small boat radars are combined with GPS but perhaps not speed log, so they are often 'ground stabilised'.

QUESTIONS

1
Q What shape would be used for a vessel at anchor?
A A Black ball/cylinder.
Q What size is the ball?
A A diameter of not less than 0.6m.
Q What about on a vessel under 20m?
A A ball diameter commensurate with the size of vessel (the ones commonly sold are 0.3m).

2
Q Identify three vessels that shall not impede in a TSS.
A Sailing vessel, vessel under 20m and a vessel engaged in fishing.
Q In a narrow channel what other vessel shall not impede?
A A vessel shall not cross a narrow channel or fairway if such a crossing impedes the passage of a vessel that can safely navigate only within that channel.

3
Q You are OOW on vessel A. You sight vessel B. What are your actions?
A Determine if a risk of collision exists by taking a series of bearings and checking if the range is decreasing on both vessels.
Q A risk of collision exists. What do you do now?
A This is a crossing situation, vessel A is the give-way, vessel B is stand-on. I would check that the area is clear, sound one short blast, make a positive turn to starboard and allow the vessel to pass. I would carefully check the effectiveness until the other vessel is finally past and clear.

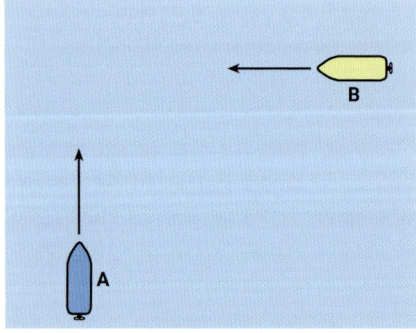

QUESTIONS

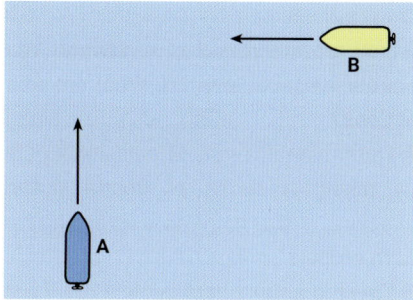

4

Q You are OOW on vessel B. You sight vessel A. What are your actions?
A Determine if a risk of collision exists by taking a series of bearings and checking if the range is decreasing on both vessels.

Q A risk of collision exists. What do you do now?
A This is a crossing situation, vessel A is the give-way, vessel B is stand-on. I would stand on and watch the other vessel's intentions.

Q The other vessel does not alter course or speed and the range is decreasing. What are your actions?
A I am now unsure of the other vessel's intentions so would sound five short blasts, stand on with caution, and ensure that my engines are ready for immediate manoeuvre.

Q The other vessel does not alter course or speed and the range is decreasing. What are your actions?
A I would take action by sounding one short blast and make a positive turn to starboard.

5

Q You are OOW on the PDV. You sight the sailing vessel. What are your actions?
A Determine if a risk of collision exists by taking a series of bearings and checking if the range is decreasing on both vessels.

Q There is a risk of collision.
A I shall keep clear as the sailing vessel has a higher priority than a PDV. I would turn to port and pass clear astern of the sailing vessel, checking the effectiveness of the manoeuvre until the other vessel is finally past and clear. I could also slow down or turn to starboard.

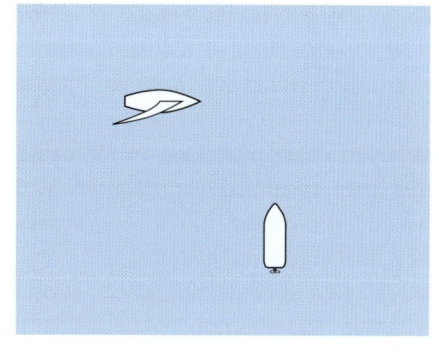

143

COLLISION REGULATIONS HANDBOOK

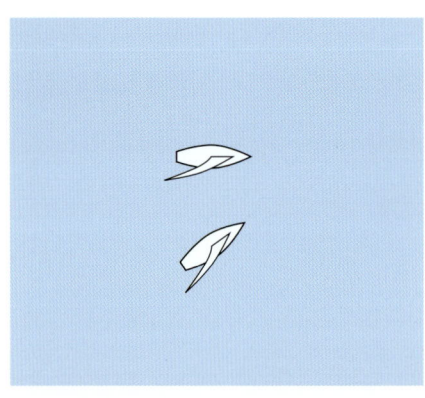

6
Q You are the vessel to windward. You sight a vessel to leeward. What are your actions?
A Determine if a risk of collision exists by taking a series of bearings and checking if the range is decreasing on both vessels.
Q There is a risk of collision.
A As the windward vessel, I am the give-way vessel, therefore I would keep clear.

7
Q You are vessel A and you are overtaking vessel B. What are your actions?
A As the overtaking vessel, it is my duty to keep clear of the vessel being overtaken. I would overtake to port or starboard while keeping clear.

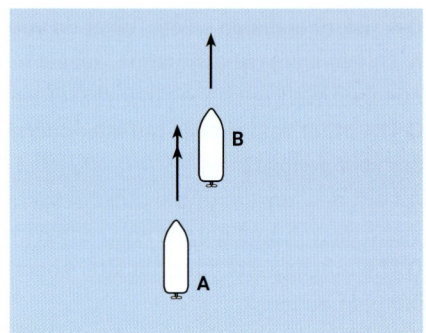

8
Q You are vessel A and you are overtaking vessel B. What are your actions?
A As the overtaking vessel, it is my duty to keep clear of the vessel being overtaken. I would overtake to starboard while keeping clear.
Q If you were overtaking to starboard and then resuming your course, you would be crossing the other vessel's bow. Is that recommended?

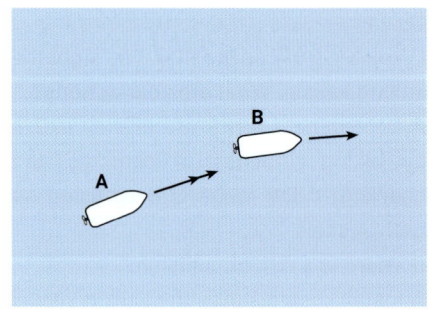

A I am able to cross in front of the other vessel, so long as my action is carried out with due regard to good seamanship. If I cross ahead of the other vessel, I am still considered the overtaking vessel and not a crossing vessel.
Note: It is sometimes easier to go astern of the vessel in an exam situation as it removes the possible conflict with crossing.

QUESTIONS

9

Q You are vessel A and you sight vessel B on your port side. What are your actions?
A Determine if a risk of collision exists by taking a series of bearings and checking if the range is decreasing on both vessels.

Q There is a risk of collision.
A I am a vessel engaged in fishing, the other vessel is a vessel restricted in her ability to manoeuvre, therefore I shall keep clear.

Q How will you keep clear?
A I have three clear options, turn to port, starboard or reduce speed.

Q Are you allowed to turn to port for a vessel on your own port side?
A Yes, because in this situation I am the give-way vessel and my only requirement is to take early and substantial action to keep well clear.

Q If those vessels were in restricted visibility, what sound signal would they make?
A Both vessels would sound one prolonged blast and two short blasts at intervals of not more than two minutes.

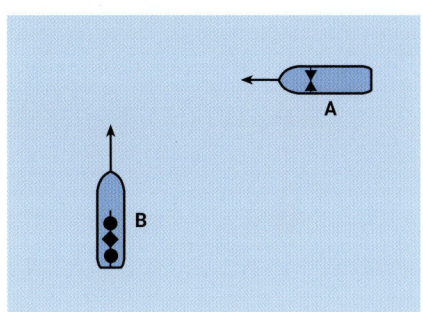

10

Q You are OOW on the bridge of vessel B. You sight vessel A. There is a risk of collision. What are your actions?
A My vessel is the vessel being overtaken; therefore, I would keep my course and speed.

Q What do the day shapes of the vessel overtaking indicate and does this change your answer?
A The day shapes mean the vessel is restricted in her ability to manoeuvre, but Rule 13 states that 'any vessel overtaking another vessel shall keep clear'.

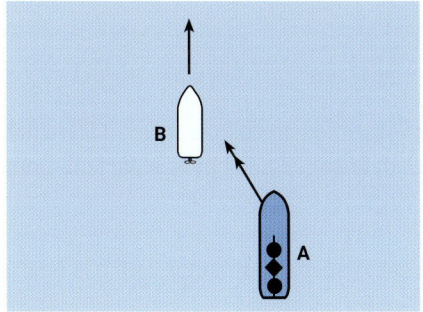

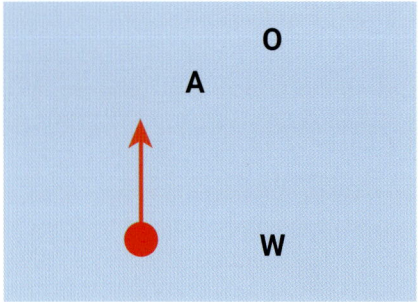

11

Q The first officer gives you this radar plot of a contact they have plotted. It is night time and the vessel is closing with a CPA that is just allowable by your standing orders. What vessel lights would you expect to see?

A The vessel will be seen approaching down the OA line and she will pass ahead of us at present. However, her actual course (WA) means that I will see a white sternlight as she passes our bow.

Q What are your actions?

A I am the overtaking vessel; therefore, I need to keep clear. If the CPA is allowable by my standing orders and my passing distance is large enough to be readily apparent to the other vessel. I would stand on with caution and continue plotting the vessel both by radar and visually.

12

Q You are the OOW on the red vessel following the traffic lane in a TSS. You sight a sailing vessel crossing. What are your actions?

A Determine if a risk of collision exists by taking a series of bearings and checking if the range is decreasing.

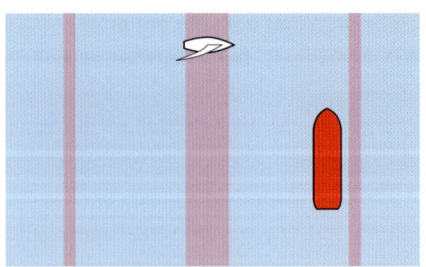

Q A risk of collision exists.

A As per priority of vessels (Rule 18), I am the give-way vessel as the other vessel is a sailing vessel. However, the sailing vessel has an obligation in a TSS to not impede my safe passage. My safe passage is not impeded and I have sufficient room to alter my course.

Q What are your intentions?

A I would slow down and allow the sailing vessel to pass and monitor until it is finally passed and clear.

QUESTIONS

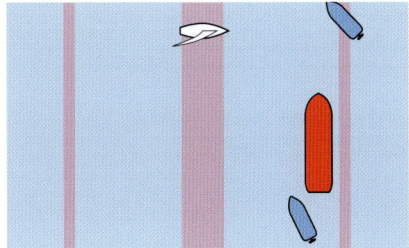

13

Q You are the OOW on the red vessel following the traffic lane in a TSS. You sight a sailing vessel crossing. A risk of collision exists. What are your actions?

A As per priority of vessels (Rule 18), I am the give-way vessel as the other vessel is a sailing vessel. However, the sailing vessel has an obligation in a TSS to not impede my safe passage. If my safe passage is impeded and I cannot alter course due to other vessels or hazards, in this case, I would stand-on with caution and watch to see if the sailing vessel allows me safe passage.

Q The sailing vessel carries on her course.

A If I am unsure of her intentions, I would sound five short blasts and watch for her intentions and have my engines and steering ready for immediate manoeuvre.

Q The sailing vessel keeps her course. What are your actions?

A I would take action by checking astern to see if the area is clear and reducing my speed to allow the sailing vessel to pass.

14

Q You are the red vessel in a narrow channel or fairway. You have a vessel crossing from your starboard side. What are your actions?

A Determine if a risk of collision exists by taking a series of bearings and checking if the range is decreasing.

Q A risk of collision exists.

A As per priority of vessels (Rule 18) I am the give-way vessel and the vessel engaged in fishing is the stand-on vessel. However, as we are in a narrow channel or fairway, the vessel engaged in fishing has an obligation not to impede my passage. Therefore, I would stand on with caution and watch the other vessel's intentions. The vessel engaged in fishing alters and passes clear.

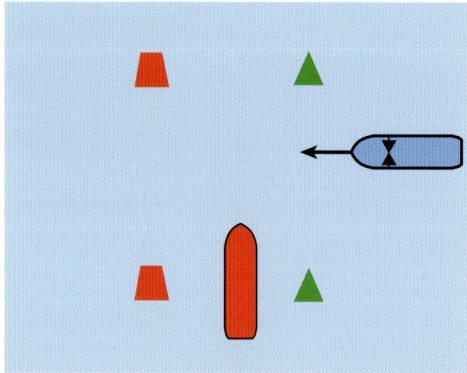

15

Q You are the red vessel in a narrow channel or fairway. You have a vessel crossing from your starboard side. A risk of collision exists. What are your actions?

A As per priority of vessels (Rule 18) I am the give-way vessel and the vessel engaged in fishing is the stand-on vessel. However, as we are in a narrow channel or fairway, the vessel engaged in fishing has an obligation not to impede my passage. I would stand on with caution and watch the other vessel's intentions.

Q The vessel engaged in fishing holds her course.

A I would sound five short blasts, watch out for her intentions and be ready to take action.

Q The vessel engaged in fishing continues on course.

A If I can only safely navigate within the confines of the channel, I would take all way off and slow down and, if necessary, make the appropriate sound signal and go astern.

Q What is the appropriate sound signal?

A Three short blasts.

QUESTIONS

16

Q Which vessels can enter the Traffic Separation Line or Zone?
A A vessel shall not normally enter a separation zone or cross a separation line except if it is a crossing vessel, a vessel joining or leaving a traffic lane, in cases of emergency or to engage in fishing.

Also, vessels restricted in their ability to manoeuvre when involved in the maintenance of the TSS are exempt from the TSS rules, as are vessels that are restricted and laying or servicing underwater cables or pipelines.

Q What are the obligations of vessels crossing the lane?
A A vessel will avoid crossing a lane, but if they do, they will cross on a heading as near as practicable at right angles to the general direction of traffic flow.

17

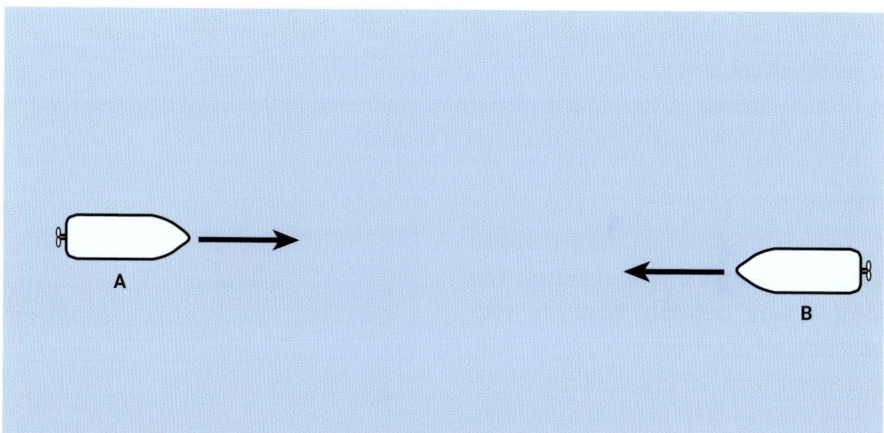

Q You are OOW on vessel B. What are your actions?
A I am a power-driven vessel and I have sighted another power-driven vessel ahead on a reciprocal or near-reciprocal course. If there is a risk of collision, I would sound one short blast and make a substantial alteration of course to starboard and pass port to port.

Q What if you are in doubt as to whether it is a head-on situation?
A If I were in doubt, I would assume it was a head-on situation and act accordingly.

18

Q You are skippering the white sailing yacht. You sight the red vessel on your port bow. What are your actions?

A Determine if a risk of collision exists by taking a series of bearings and checking if the range is decreasing.

Q A risk of collision exists.

A The white vessel has the wind on her port side; therefore, I will keep out of the way of the sailing yacht with the wind on her starboard side.

Q What will you do?

A I could slow down, turn to port or hard to starboard. In this circumstance, I would most likely turn to port if the wind direction allowed.

19

Q You are the OOW on the red vessel following the traffic lane in a TSS. You sight a ferry crossing. What are your actions?

A Determine if a risk of collision exists by taking a series of bearings and checking if the range is decreasing.

Q A risk of collision exists.

A The normal collision regulations apply while in the TSS, therefore it is a

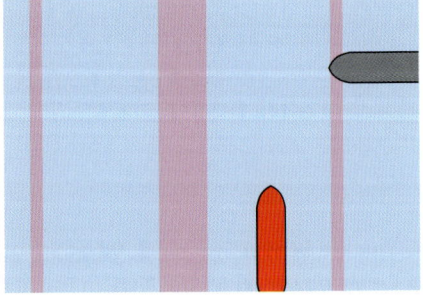

crossing situation. I am the give-way vessel, so I would sound one short blast and turn to starboard, or slow down and allow the other vessel to pass.

Q Would this mean that you would enter the ITZ?

A It may, depending on the size of the lane, but this is allowed to avoid immediate danger.

QUESTIONS

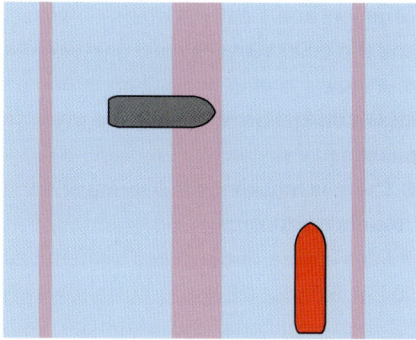

20

Q You are the OOW on the red vessel following the traffic lane in a TSS. You sight a ferry crossing. What are your actions?

A Determine if a risk of collision exists by taking a series of bearings and checking if the range is decreasing.

Q A risk of collision exists.

A The normal collision regulations apply while in the TSS, therefore it is a crossing situation and I am the stand-on vessel and the other vessel should give way.

Q There is no change in bearing and the vessels are closing.

A I am unsure of the vessel's intentions so I would sound five short blasts, watch for its intentions and stand on with caution, ensuring my engines are ready for immediate manoeuvre.

Q There is no change in bearing and the vessels are closing.

A I would make a navigational assessment of the vessels around me and slow my vessel to allow the other to pass.

Q What about if there were vessels astern of you?

A I would sound one short blast and make a substantial turn to starboard and monitor the other vessel until she passes clear. Once clear I would regain the traffic lane at a shallow angle and report the incident to the TSS controlling station.

Q Could you go behind the other vessel?

A No, that would entail a turn to port for a vessel on my own port side.

21

Q You are the OOW on the red vessel following the traffic lane in a TSS. You sight a small 12m motor vessel crossing. What are your actions?

A Determine if a risk of collision exists by taking a series of bearings and checking if the range is decreasing.

Q A risk of collision exists.

A The normal collision regulations apply while in the TSS, therefore it is a crossing

COLLISION REGULATIONS HANDBOOK

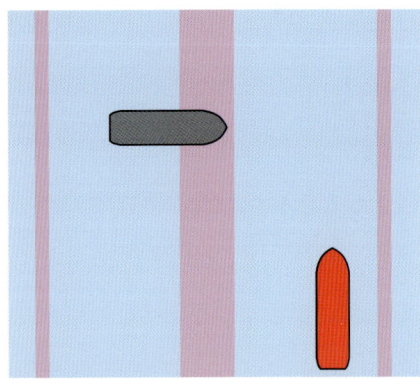

situation and I am the stand-on vessel and the other vessel should give way. As this vessel is also under 20m, it has an added obligation not to impede my safe passage.

Q There is no change in bearing and the vessels are closing.

A I am unsure of the vessel's intentions so I would sound five short blasts, watch for her intentions and stand on with caution, ensuring my engines are ready for immediate manoeuvre.

The other vessel has heard your sound signal, turns to port and allows you to pass.

22

Q You are Master on the red vessel in a narrow channel or fairway. You sight a ferry on your starboard bow. What are your actions?

A Determine if a risk of collision exists by taking a series of bearings and checking if the range is decreasing.

Q A risk of collision exists.

A This is a crossing situation; however, a vessel shall not cross a narrow channel if such a crossing impedes the passage of a vessel that can only navigate in the

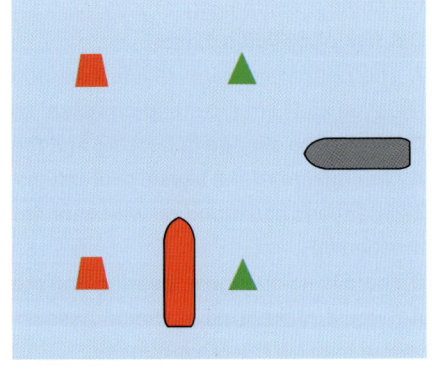

channel. If I can only safely navigate within the channel, I would sound five short blasts as I'm unsure of the ferry's intentions.

Q There is no response from the crossing vessel and the distance is closing.

A I would reduce my speed to a minimum and allow the other vessel to cross ahead as I am still the give-way vessel.

23

Q Upon whom do the Collision Regulations place responsibilities?

A The owner, Master and crew.

24

Q What can be used to exonerate the owner, Master or crew from compliance with the ColRegs?

QUESTIONS

A Nothing. Nothing shall exonerate the owner, Master or crew from the consequences of any neglect to comply with these Rules or of the neglect of any precaution that may be required by the ordinary practice of seamen.

25
Q Is there a time when you do not need to follow the ColRegs at sea?
A No. However, I may make a departure from these Rules in special circumstances and if necessary to avoid immediate danger. If I do make this departure, necessary to avoid immediate danger, I will still comply.

26
Q What is the difference between a vessel Not Under Command and a vessel Restricted in her Ability to Manoeuvre?
A The term 'vessel restricted in her ability to manoeuvre' means a vessel that from the nature of her work is restricted in her ability to manoeuvre and is therefore unable to keep out of the way of another vessel. The term 'vessel not under command' means a vessel that through some exceptional circumstance is unable to manoeuvre and is therefore unable to keep out of the way of another vessel.

27
Q What is meant by the term 'underway'?
A The term 'underway' means that a vessel is not at anchor, or made fast to the shore, or aground. Therefore, it would be drifting and moving with the stream and wind.

28
Q What is meant by the term 'making way'?
A There is no definition of 'making way' in the ColRegs. However, it is mentioned in the lights section (underway and making way) and in the sounds section for vessels in restricted visibility. If underway means not made fast – making way would best be described as in gear and en route to the destination.

29
Q What vessels would you expect to be Restricted in their Ability to Manoeuvre?
A A vessel engaged in laying, servicing or picking up a navigation mark, submarine cable or pipeline;
A vessel engaged in dredging, surveying or underwater operations;
A vessel engaged in replenishment or transferring persons, provisions or cargo while underway;
A vessel engaged in the launching or recovery of aircraft;
A vessel engaged in mine clearance operations;

A vessel engaged in a towing operation such as severely restricts the towing vessel and her tow in their ability to deviate from their course.

30

Q What is a rowing boat termed as, within the rules?
A A vessel under oars is only mentioned in lights. However, in normal circumstances she would be classed as a power-driven vessel as she is propelled by machinery, albeit manual machinery (oars). She would be lit as per the section in lights.

31

Q As OOW in restricted visibility, you sight a contact fine on the port bow at 4½ miles. What are your actions?
A If this was the first sighting of the contact, I would stand on and continue plotting. At present, a single contact is scanty information and I cannot say that a close-quarters situation is developing or risk of collision exists.
Q At what intervals would you manually plot?
A Normally six-minute intervals, but if we or the other vessel were closing faster, three-minute intervals.

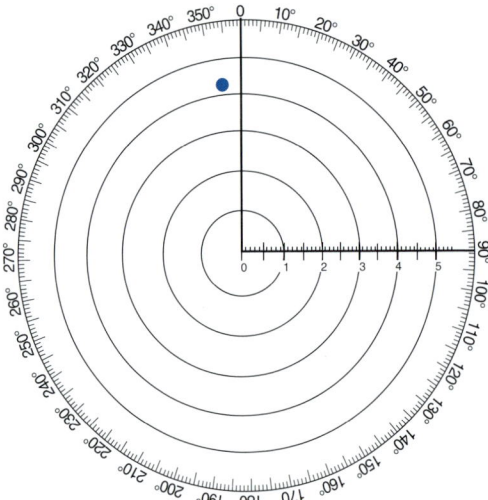

QUESTIONS

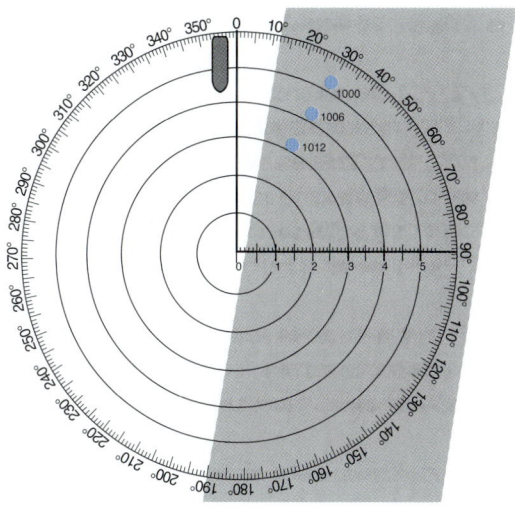

32

Q As OOW you view two vessels ahead – one observed visually fine on your port bow and another contact on radar three points off your starboard bow, which is in an area of restricted visibility. What are your actions?

A Determine if a risk of collision exists by taking a series of bearings and checking if the range is decreasing on both vessels. I can see that we have a series of plots giving a close CPA. I would monitor the vessel ahead as her intentions presently are head-on, but I would continue to monitor before making a decision.

Q A risk of collision exists with both. What are your actions?

A The vessel ahead, even though she is near restricted visibility, is observed visually and in a head-on situation. Therefore, I would turn to starboard.

The vessel in restricted visibility is observed by radar, therefore I would use Rule 19(d)(i) and I would avoid turning to port. Therefore, in this instance, I'd turn to starboard.

> In the following questions, the red and the blue arrows indicate a vessel's True heading. The length of the arrow indicates the vessel's speed/distance travelled in six minutes.

33

Q On a clear night, as OOW you observe a contact on your starboard quarter by radar. What are your actions?

A Determine if a risk of collision exists by taking a series of bearings and checking if the range is decreasing.

155

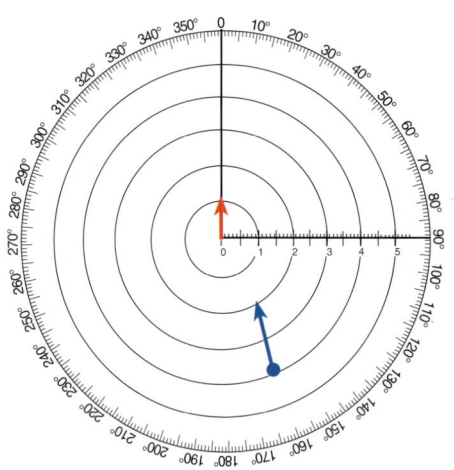

Q A risk of collision does exist.
A This is an overtaking situation and my obligation is to keep my course and speed.
The other vessel passes clear.

34

Q On a clear night, as OOW you observe a contact on your starboard quarter by radar. What are your actions?
A Determine if a risk of collision exists by taking a series of bearings and checking if the range is decreasing.

Q A risk of collision does exist.
A This is an overtaking situation and my obligation is to keep my course and speed.

Q The other vessel has not made any alteration and a risk of collision still exists.
A I would signal to the other vessel that I am unsure of her intentions with five short blasts, supplemented with five light flashes.

Q The other vessel continues to approach and has not altered their course.
A I would increase speed to give more time to assess the situation. I would then continue to monitor, but the situation may have now passed and it is likely the other vessel has now passed astern of me.

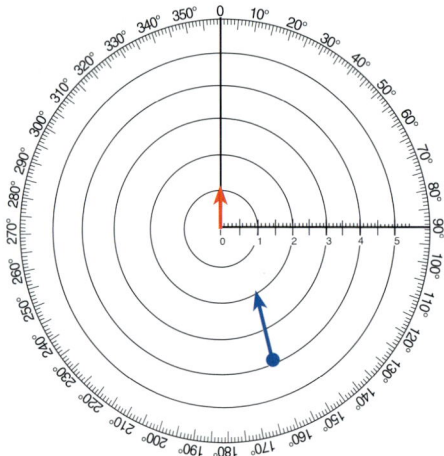

QUESTIONS

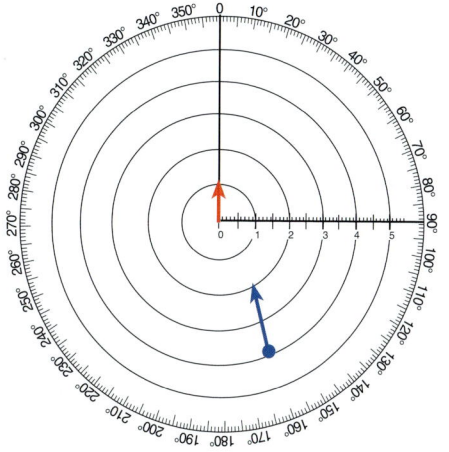

In the following questions, the red and the blue arrows indicate a vessel's relative heading. The length of the arrow indicates the vessel's speed/distance travelled in 6 minutes.

35

Q In fog, as OOW you observe a contact on your starboard quarter by radar. What are your actions?

A Determine if a risk of collision exists by taking a series of plots and checking if the range is decreasing.

Q A risk of collision does exist.

A As this is restricted visibility, I would not turn towards a vessel abeam or abaft the beam, so in this case I would turn to port.

Q What would you expect the other vessel to do?

A As I am forward of its beam and the other vessel is overtaking, I would expect the other vessel to turn to starboard or port or slow down.

Q Why, as we are forward of its beam, can the other vessel turn to port?

A Because Rule 19(d)(i) allows a turn to port for a vessel forward of the beam being overtaken.

36

Q How would you determine a risk of collision by radar?

A I would systematically plot the other vessel's position. This could be by manual plotting, use of the Electronic Bearing Line (EBL) or ARPA/MARPA.

37

Q In fog, as OOW you observe a contact three points off your port bow by radar. What are your actions?

A Determine if a risk of collision exists by taking a series of plots and checking if the range is decreasing.

Q A risk of collision does exist.

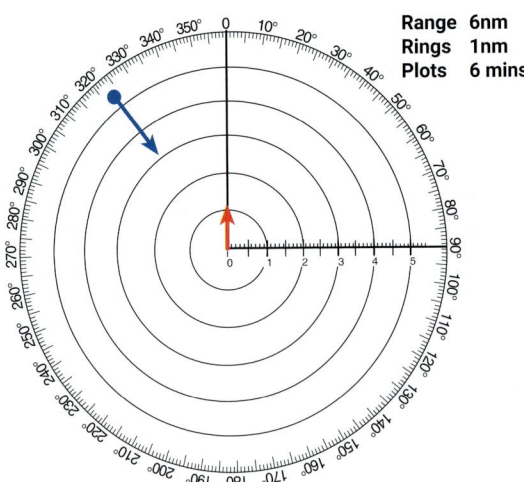

Range 6nm
Rings 1nm
Plots 6 mins

A As this is restricted visibility, I would not turn to port for a vessel forward of the beam, so in this case I would turn to starboard.

Q What would you expect the other vessel to do?

A Most probably turn to starboard.

38

Q In fog, as OOW you observe a contact on your starboard beam by radar. What are your actions?

A Determine if a risk of collision exists by taking a series of plots and checking if the range is decreasing.

Q A risk of collision does exist.

A As this is restricted visibility, I would not turn towards a vessel abeam or abaft the beam, therefore I would turn to port.

Q Before turning to port, would you sound your intentions prior to doing so?

A No. Manoeuvring signals are only allowed when in sight of one another.

Q What signal would you sound?

A If I were a power-driven vessel under and making way, one prolonged blast at intervals not exceeding two minutes.

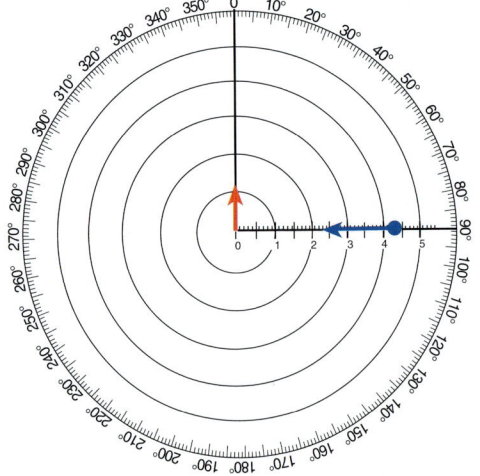

QUESTIONS

39

Q You are the red vessel in a narrow channel or fairway and there is a vessel intending to overtake. What would you expect to happen?

A I would expect the overtaking vessel to seek permission from me to overtake. It looks like she is intending to overtake on my port side, so I would expect her to sound two prolonged blasts, followed by two short blasts.

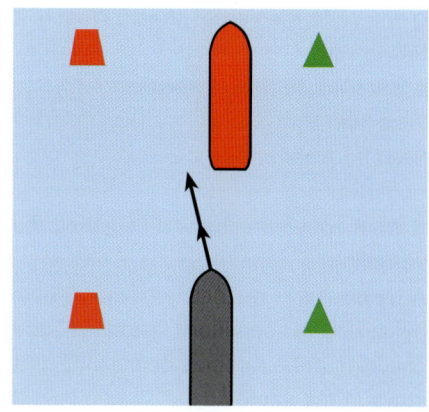

Q What would your reply be if you consider her safe to pass?

A Long, short, long, short blasts.

Q How far to starboard would you take your vessel?

A I would stay as far to starboard as practicable, taking into account depth of water, under-keel clearance, wind and drift, etc. However, the responsibility is for the other vessel to keep clear.

40

Q You are OOW on the grey vessel. What are your actions?

A I am approaching a bend and I will sound one long blast to alert other vessels of my presence.

Q What would you expect the other vessel to do?

A Sound a similar one long blast.

Q How would you conduct your vessel?

A Stay as far to starboard as practicable.

Q Would you be able to sound this signal in restricted visibility?

A Yes, it can alert vessels in any state of visibility.

41

Q You sight the vessel ahead. What is it telling you?
A It is a power-driven vessel.
Less than 50m.
Seen from ahead.
Underway.

Q What are your actions on sighting the vessel?
A Determine if a risk of collision exists by taking a series of bearings and checking if the range is decreasing. If it stays at the same aspect, it is a vessel approaching head on.

Q The aspect stays the same and the range is decreasing.
A I would sound one short blast, supplemented by a light signal, and turn to starboard, passing port to port with the other vessel.

42

Q As OOW you sight a vessel three points off your port bow. What is it telling you?
A It is a power-driven vessel.
Under 50m.
Starboard aspect.
Engaged in towing.
With a length of tow over 200m.

Q What are your intentions?
A Determine if a risk of collision exists by taking a series of bearings and checking if the range is decreasing.

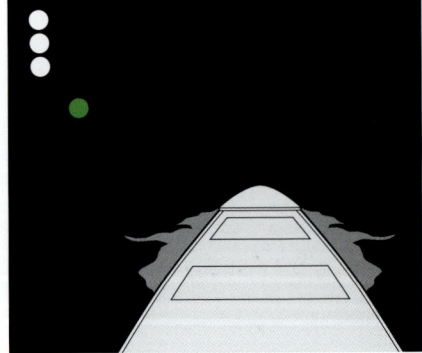

Q A risk of collision exists.
A This is a crossing situation and I am the stand-on vessel. Therefore, I would stand on and watch for the other vessel's intentions.

Q Does the vessel engaged in towing have a higher priority than a power-driven vessel?
A No – it is not showing RAM lights.

43

Q As OOW you sight a vessel three points off your port bow. What is it telling you?
A It is a power-driven vessel.
Under 50m.
Starboard aspect.
Engaged in towing.
With a length of tow over 200m.
Restricted in her ability to manoeuvre.

Q What are your intentions?
A Determine if a risk of collision exists by taking a series of bearings and checking if the range is decreasing.

Q A risk of collision exists.
A As the vessel is restricted in her ability to manoeuvre, my responsibility is to keep clear.

Q What are your actions?
A My action in this circumstance would be to slow down and let the other vessel pass ahead.

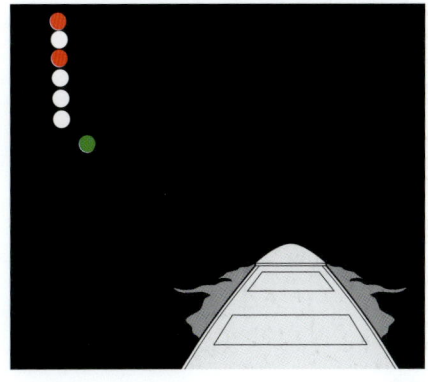

44

Q What do the lights on this vessel indicate?
A This vessel is not under command.
Underway but not making way.

Q What lights would she use to state that she was making way?
A Sidelights and a sternlight.

Q If you saw this vessel ahead, what would be your actions?
A Determine if a risk of collision exists by taking a series of bearings and checking if the range is decreasing.

Q A risk of collision exists.
A Make a bold alteration of course to port or starboard and pass well clear.

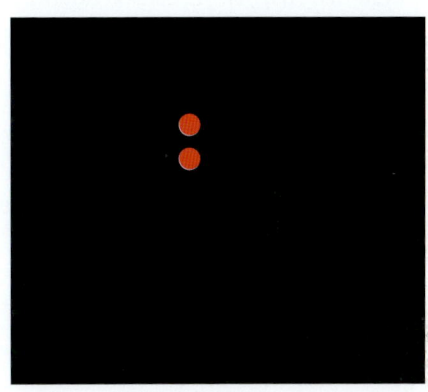

45

Q What do the lights on this vessel indicate?

A This is the stern view of a vessel engaged in towing.

Q What size of vessel is she and how long is the tow?

A There is no indication of length of vessel or tow.

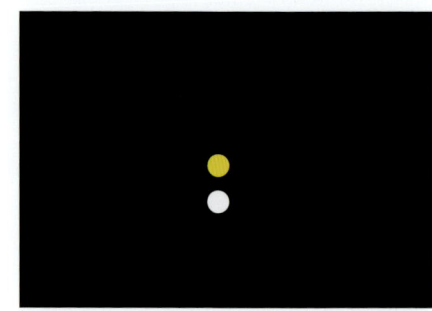

46

Q What do the lights on this vessel indicate?

A This vessel is engaged in fishing.
Making way.
Starboard aspect.
Gear extending over 150m.

Q What are your actions?

A Determine if a risk of collision exists by taking a series of bearings and checking if the range is decreasing.

Q A risk of collision exists.

A As the other vessel is engaged in fishing I would give way, by either making a substantial turn to starboard or port or slowing down. If I passed behind the vessel, I would remember that she has outlying gear over 150m.

47

Q What do the lights on this vessel indicate?

A This vessel is restricted in her ability to manoeuvre.
Engaged in underwater operations.
Clear to pass on the green side, obstruction on the red side.

Q What lights would this vessel show when she is at anchor?

A This vessel would not show anchor lights when involved in underwater operations.

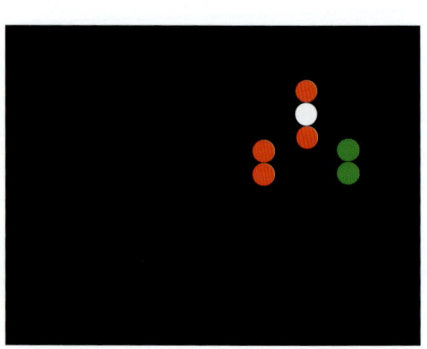

QUESTIONS

48

Q What do the lights on this vessel indicate?

A This vessel is restricted in her ability to manoeuvre.
Not making way.

Q Is it at anchor?

A No. A vessel restricted in her ability to manoeuvre would show an anchor light, unless she was engaged in minesweeping or dredging/underwater operations.

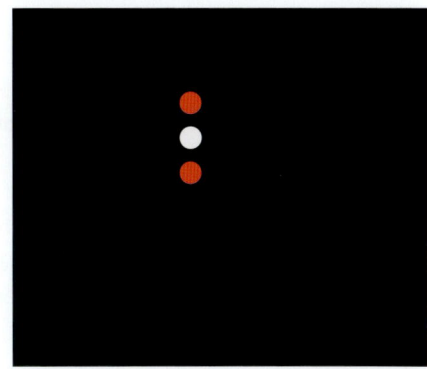

49

Q What do the lights on this vessel indicate?

A This vessel is a power-driven vessel, probably over 50m in length.
Port aspect.
Constrained by her draught.

Q What are your actions?

A Determine if a risk of collision exists by taking a series of bearings and checking if the range is decreasing.

Q A risk of collision exists.

A I am the give-way vessel and as the other vessel is a power-driven vessel, this is a crossing situation. As the other vessel is constrained by her draught, I have an added obligation not to impede her safe passage. I would make my intention clear and either reduce speed or turn to starboard and go behind the vessel.

50

Q What does the light on this vessel indicate?

A It could be a number of vessels:
A sternlight.
At anchor under 50m.
Sailing vessel under 7m.
Vessel under oars.
Power-driven vessel less than 7m and doing less than 7 knots.

51

Q In restricted visibility you hear the following sound signal ahead, what are your actions?
A If I have been tracking the other vessel by radar and know that she will pass clear I will carry on with caution. However, if I am uncertain, I would reduce my speed to the minimum at which I can be kept on course. I shall, if necessary, take all my way off and in any event navigate with extreme caution until danger of collision is over.

52

Q In restricted visibility you hear the following signal. What is it?
A It is a power-driven vessel, underway, but not making way, engaged in pilotage duties.
Q What lights would she show in this state?
A Two all-round lights, white over red, with sidelights and a sternlight.

53

Q You are a power-driven vessel in restricted visibility, making way. What sound signal would you make?
A One prolonged blast, at intervals of not more than two minutes.
Q How long is the long blast?
A Four to six seconds.

54

Q You are a power-driven vessel making way in restricted visibility and by radar alone you have been tracking a vessel forward of the beam that you have established a close-quarters situation exists. What are your actions?
A As a risk exists, I would avoid a turn to port. Therefore, I would turn to starboard.
Q What sound signal would you make when turning to starboard?
A No manoeuvring signal as these are only used by vessels in sight of one another. However, I would continue to sound one prolonged blast at intervals not exceeding two minutes.

55

Q You are a power-driven vessel in restricted visibility and by radar you have been tracking a vessel forward of the beam that is coming from your starboard side and

you have established that a risk of collision exists. At about one mile, sight of the vessel's lights confirm this. What are your actions?
A As a risk of collision exists, I would make a positive alteration of course, ensuring that my intentions are clear to the other vessel.
Q What sound signal would you make if turning to starboard?
A One short blast, supplemented at night by a single flash.
Q Can you make such a signal in restricted visibility?
A Yes, as I am now in sight of the other vessel.

56

Q You are running along a coast and approaching a harbour area in restricted visibility, when you hear the above sound signal: What are your actions?
A This sound would be from a vessel at anchor that was unsure if an approaching vessel was going to pass clear. I would reduce speed and be prepared to take all way off, review radar information, check my position and redouble my efforts to listen for anchor signals.
Q If the vessel was over 100m, what signals would you expect to hear?
A A bell in the fore part for five seconds, followed immediately after by a gong in the aft part for five seconds.
Q At what interval would you expect this?
A At intervals not exceeding one minute.

57

Q You are joining a vessel in a port with which you are unfamiliar. You hear sound signals that are not familiar to you being used by vessels. What is going on?
A The Collision Regulations in Rule 1 allow harbours and ports to modify sound and lights to best suit their purpose for vessels in their waters.
Q Where would you find out the information in the port?
A The port or harbour byelaws would be my first choice, followed by contacting the Port Authority for guidance if I was unclear.

58

Q In restricted visibility, you hear the signal of one long blast, two short blasts, followed closely by one long blast, three short blasts astern of you. What is the vessel?
A The one long, two short blasts is a vessel towing and the one long, three short is the vessel towed or the last vessel in the tow, if manned.
Q What are your actions?

A As the vessel is astern of me and I am in restricted visibility, I would keep my course and speed as the vessel is not ahead of me. I would also retune my radar and post additional look-outs aft and continue with caution sounding the appropriate signal, while continuing to determine whether a close-quarters situation or risk of collision is developing.

59
Q In restricted visibility you hear the signal of one long blast and two short blasts ahead of you. What is that signal telling you?
A It could be any of the following vessels:
Not under command;
Restricted in ability to manoeuvre;
Constrained by draught;
Towing or pushing;
Vessel engaged in fishing;
Sailing vessel.
Q What are your actions?
A Unless I have been able to ascertain that a risk of collision does not exist, I would reduce my speed and be prepared to take all way off until I establish that risk of collision is over.
Q Would your actions be any different if it were one prolonged blast?
A No. Rule 19(e) does not differentiate between vessels.

60
Q In harbour, when exiting a dock, you hear three short blasts. What does this signify?
A It is a vessel operating astern propulsion.
Q What are your actions?
A Ask the bridge team to look around for a vessel either reversing or slowing, listen to the Port operations channel on the VHF, and carry on with caution.

61
Q List five methods we would use to determine a safe speed.
A By all vessels:
- The state of visibility;
- The traffic density, including concentrations of fishing vessels or any other vessels;
- The manoeuvrability of the vessel with special reference to stopping distance and turning ability in the prevailing conditions;
- At night the presence of background light such as from shore lights or from back scatter of her own lights;
- The state of wind, sea and current, and the proximity of navigational hazards;
- The draught in relation to the available depth of water.

QUESTIONS

62
Q You are the red vessel in open water and you observe a vessel on your port side. What are your actions?
A Determine if a risk of collision exists by taking a series of bearings and checking if the range is decreasing.
Q A risk of collision exists.
A I am a power-driven vessel. Therefore, I have to keep clear of the vessel engaged in fishing. However, the vessel engaged in fishing has an obligation not to impede my safe passage as I am showing the day shape of constrained by draught. Therefore, initially I would stand on and watch for her intentions.
Q The vessel engaged in fishing stands on.
A Depending on the circumstances, I would sound five short blasts and watch for her intentions.
Q The vessel engaged in fishing stands on.
A I would slow my vessel and allow the other vessel to pass as I am unable to deviate from my course.

63
Q What does 'restricted visibility' mean?
A The term 'restricted visibility' means any condition in which visibility is restricted by fog, mist, falling snow, heavy rainstorms, sandstorms or any other similar causes.

64
Q You come on to the bridge to take over the watch from the OOW. The OOW is in the middle of a manoeuvre to avoid a situation. What are your actions?
A Let the OOW finish the manoeuvre and then take over after appraising the situation.

65
Q When taking action to avoid a close-quarters situation with another vessel, how much would you alter course?
A It should be large enough to be readily apparent to another vessel, observing visually or by radar.

66
Q You are OOW on the bridge and the Master is in their bunk. What are your responsibilities?
A The nominated OOW or Watchkeeper is the Master's representative and is primarily responsible at all times for the safe navigation of the ship and for complying with the

167

ColRegs. The lead OOW may oversee other officers on the bridge, depending on the vessel size and make-up.

67

Q What are the responsibilities of the look-out?
A Maintaining a continuous state of vigilance by sight and hearing, as well as by all other available means.
Fully appraising the situation and the risk of collision, stranding and other dangers to navigation.
Detecting ships or aircraft in distress, shipwrecked persons, wrecks, debris and other hazards to safe navigation.

68

Q What is the meaning of this flag?
A I have a diver down.
Q What size should it be?
A 1m in height.
Q What is its construction?
A Rigid replica of an A flag to ensure all-round visibility.

69

Q You are approaching some harbour approaches and sight these lights ahead. What is it?
A This is a vessel at anchor, over 50m, starboard aspect (higher light being near the bow).
Q What are your actions?
A I would check my position and avoid the vessel, probably going around her stern, if there is sufficient water.

70

Q You are a power-driven vessel at night underway and making way. You get to your work area and you stop making way and are now underway. What changes do you make to your lights?
A None. A power-driven vessel does not change her lights when going from making way to underway.

71

Q You sight this vessel on your port bow at night. What is it?
A It is a sailing vessel. Starboard aspect with no indication of length.

QUESTIONS

Q You are a power-driven vessel, what are your actions?
A Determine if a risk of collision exists by taking a series of bearings and checking if the range is decreasing.
Q The bearing is constant and range decreasing.
A My obligation is to keep clear. Therefore, I would sound two short blasts and make a positive alteration to port.

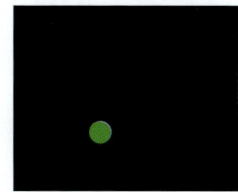

72

Q You see these lights ahead of you, with risk of collision. What are they and what are your actions?
A This is a power-driven vessel constrained by her draught. I can see her stern. I am the overtaking vessel, therefore, I would keep out of the way.

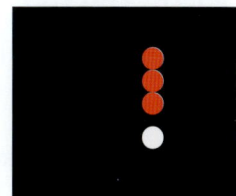

73

Q You sight these lights ahead of you. What is it?
A A vessel aground, port aspect, over 50m.
Q What are your actions?
A Check my chart and most probably slow down and plot a course to clear the vessel in safe water.

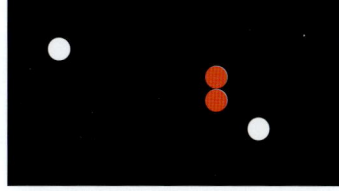

74

Q You see this vessel ahead of you. What are your actions?
A If it is head-on and coming towards me, I would sound one short blast and make a positive alteration of course to starboard.
Q What would you expect the other vessel to do?
A Her responsibility would be to also turn to starboard.
Q What is the other vessel?
A It is a power-driven vessel, under 50m, towing another vessel alongside.
Q Does this vessel have any greater rights over your power-driven vessel?
A No, as she is not displaying restricted in ability to manoeuvre. However, I would ensure my actions were made in ample time and with due regard to good seamanship.

75

Q What sections of the ColRegs are applied in restricted visibility?
A Section I – Conduct of vessels in any conditions of visibility and Section III – Conduct of vessels in restricted visibility.

APPENDICES

MGN 324 (M+F) Amendment 2

Operational guidance on the use of VHF radio and Automatic Identification Systems at Sea

1. Introduction/background

1.1 The International Maritime Organization (IMO) and wider maritime community noted with concern the widespread misuse of VHF channels at sea, especially the distress, safety and calling Channels 16 (156.8 MHz) and 70 (156.525 MHz), and channels used for port operations, ship movement services and reporting systems. Although at sea VHF makes an important contribution to navigation safety, its misuse causes serious interference and, in itself, becomes a danger to safety at sea. IMO Member Governments have unanimously agreed to ensure that VHF channels are used appropriately and correctly.

1.2 It should be borne in mind that not all ships or marine craft carry or are required to carry AIS. The officer of the watch (OOW) should always be aware that other ships, in particular leisure craft, fishing vessels and warships, and some coastal shore stations, including Vessel Traffic Service (VTS) centres, might not be fitted with AIS.

1.3 The OOW should always be aware that AIS fitted on other vessels as a mandatory carriage requirement, might, under certain circumstances, be switched off on the Master's discretion and professional judgement. Users are, therefore, cautioned always to bear in mind that information provided by AIS may not be giving a complete or correct "picture" of shipping traffic in their vicinity.

2. VHF Communications and usage

2.1 All users of marine VHF on United Kingdom vessels and all other vessels in UK territorial waters and in vicinity of harbours are reminded in conformance with international and national legislation, that marine VHF equipment may only be used in accordance with the ITU Radio Regulations. These Regulations specifically prescribe that:

2.1.1 Channel 16 may only be used for distress, urgency and very brief safety communications, and for calling to establish other communications which should then be concluded on a suitable working channel;

2.1.2 Channel 70 may only be used for Digital Selective Calling, not oral communication;

APPENDICES

2.1.3 On VHF channels allocated to port operations or ship movement services, such as VTS, the only messages permitted are restricted to those relating to operational handling, the movement and the safety of ships and to the safety of persons;

2.1.4 All transmissions must be preceded by an identification, for example the vessel's name or call sign; and

2.1.5 The service of every VHF radio telephone station must be controlled by an operator holding a certificate issued or recognised by the station's controlling Administration. This is usually the country of registration, if the vessel is registered. Provided that the Station is so controlled, other persons besides the holder of the certificate may use the equipment.

2.2 Channels 6, 8, 72 and 77 have been made available, in UK waters, for routine ship-to-ship communications, Masters, Skippers and Owners are urged to ensure that all ship-to-ship communications working in these waters is confined to these channels, selecting the channel most appropriate in the local conditions at the time.

2.3 Channel 13 is designated for use on a worldwide basis as a navigation safety communication channel, primarily for inter-ship navigation safety communications. It may also be used for the ship movement and port services.

2.4 IMO Resolution A.954(23), Proper use of VHF Channels at Sea, should be consulted. To get indicative information on typical VHF communication ranges, the section - "The Management of VHF" - within Admiralty List of Radio Signals Volume 5, published by the United Kingdom Hydrographic Office, may be referred.

3. Use of VHF to Aid Collision Avoidance

3.1 There have been a significant number of collisions where subsequent investigations have found that at some stage before impact, one or both parties were using VHF radio in an attempt to avoid collision. The use of VHF radio in these circumstances is not always helpful and may even prove to be dangerous.

3.2 At night, in restricted visibility or when there are more than two vessels in the vicinity, the need for positive identification is essential but this can rarely be guaranteed. Uncertainties can arise over the identification of vessels, correlation and interpretation of messages received. Even where positive identification has been achieved there is still the possibility of a misunderstanding due to language difficulties however fluent the parties concerned might be in the language being used. An imprecise or ambiguously expressed message could have serious consequences.

3.3 Valuable time can be wasted whilst mariners on vessels approaching each other try to make contact on VHF radio instead of complying with the COLREG. There is the further danger that even if contact and identification are achieved and no difficulties over the language of communication or message content arise, a course of action might still be chosen that does not comply with the COLREG. This may lead to the collision it was intended to prevent.

3.4 In 1995, the judge in a collision case said -"It is very probable that the use of VHF radio for conversation between these ships was a contributory cause of this collision, if only because it distracted the officers on watch from paying careful attention to their radar. I must repeat, in the hope that it will achieve some publicity, what I have said on previous occasions that any attempt to use VHF to agree the manner of passing is fraught with the danger of misunderstanding. Marine Superintendents would be well advised to prohibit such use of VHF radio and to instruct their officers to comply with the Collision Regulations."

3.5 In a case published in 2002, one of two vessels, approaching each other in fog, used the VHF radio to call for a red to red (port to port) passing. The call was acknowledged by the other vessel but unfortunately, due to the command of English on the calling vessel, what the caller intended was a green to green (starboard to starboard) passing. The actions were not effectively monitored by either of the vessels and collision ensued.

3.6 Again, in a case published in 2006 one of two vessels, approaching one another involving a close quarter's situation, agreed to a starboard to starboard passing arrangement with a person on board another, unidentified ship, but not the approaching vessel. Furthermore, the passing agreement required one of the vessels to make an alteration of course contrary to the requirements of the applicable Rule in the COLREG. Had the vessel agreed to a passing arrangement requiring her to manoeuvre in compliance with the COLREG, the ships would have passed clear, despite the misidentification of ships on the VHF radio. Unfortunately, by the time both vessels realised that the ships had turned towards each other the distance between them had further reduced to the extent that the last-minute avoiding action taken by both ships was unable to prevent a collision.

3.7 More recently, in 2014, inappropriate use of VHF radios was highlighted as a major factor in collision between a bulk carrier and container ship which occurred in open sea with very sparse traffic around the vessels. Navigating officers on both vessels relied solely on the VHF for collision avoidance decision to negotiate a manoeuvre that was contrary to the COLREG. To further complicate the matter, VHF radio communications were not conducted in English which was both of the ships' working language, and which confused a relieving officer on one of the vessels who was not able to understand what had been tacitly agreed via the VHF communications.

3.8 Although the practice of using VHF radio as a collision avoidance aid may be resorted to on occasion, for example in pilotage waters, the risks described in this Guidance Note should be clearly understood and the COLREG complied with to their best possible extent.

4. Use of Automatic Identification System (AIS)

4.1 AIS operates primarily on two dedicated VHF channels (AIS1 – 161.975 MHz; and AIS2 – 162.025 MHz). Where these channels are not available regionally, the AIS is capable of automatically switching to alternate designated channels. AIS has now been installed on the majority of commercial vessels and has the potential to make a significant contribution to safety. However, the mariner should treat the AIS information with caution, noting the following important points.

4.2 Mariners on craft fitted with AIS should be aware that the AIS will be transmitting ownship data to other vessels and shore stations.

To this end they are advised to:
- initiate action to correct any known improper installation;
- ensure the correct information on the vessel's identity, position, and movements (including voyage-specific) is transmitted; and
- ensure that the AIS, if being off for any reason, is turned on, at least within 100 nautical miles of the coastline of the United Kingdom.

4.3 The simplest means of checking whether ownship is transmitting correct information on identity, position and movements is by contacting other vessels or shore stations. Increasingly, UK maritime rescue coordination centres and port authorities are being equipped as AIS base stations. As more base stations are established ashore, AIS may be used to provide a functional monitoring system in conjunction with Vessel Traffic Services and Ship Reporting (SOLAS Chapter V, Regulations 11 and 12 refer).

4.4 Many ship owners have opted for the least-cost AIS installation to meet the mandatory carriage requirement. By doing so many of the benefits offered by graphic display (especially AIS overlaid on radar) are not realised with the 3-line 'Minimum Keyboard Display' (MKD), although the unit may still be duly type approved.

4.5 It is becoming common practice for pilots to possess their own portable navigational equipment which they carry on board. Such devices can be connected to shipborne AIS equipment and display the targets they receive. This, so called, Pilot Connector Socket and suitable power outlet should be located somewhere of practical use to a marine pilot who may carry compatible AIS equipment. This should be somewhere close to the wheelhouse main conning position. Less accessible locations in chart rooms, e.g. at the after end of the wheelhouse are not recommended.

4.6 The routine updating of data into the AIS, at the start of the voyage and whenever changes occur, should be covered in the navigating officer's checklist and should consist of:
- ship's draught;
- hazardous cargo, if any;
- destination and ETA;
- route plan (way points);
- correct navigational status; and
- short safety-related messages.

4.7 The quality and reliability of position data obtained from targets will vary depending on the accuracy of the transmitting vessel's Electronic Position Fixing System (EPFS) receiver. It should be noted that older EPFS equipment (before 2003) may not produce Course Over Ground and Speed Over Ground (COG/SOG) data to the same accuracy as newer equipment.

4.8 IMO Resolution A.1106(29), Revised Guidelines for the Onboard Operational Use of Shipborne Automatic Identification Systems (AIS), published December 2015, should be consulted for better understanding of the operational functions and limitations of the AIS.

Use of AIS to Support Safety of Navigation

4.9 Modern radar and ECDIS units (installed onboard on or after 1 July 2008) have provisions for AIS integration which is able to 'overlay' additional information on the radar and ECDIS displays. However, this also implies that there will be older AIS "stand alone" units without integration to other displays.

4.10 On the vessels with integrated AIS and radar, if the target data from AIS and radar tracking are both available, and if the target association criteria (for example position, motion) are fulfilled such that the AIS and radar information are considered as one physical target, the activated AIS target symbol and the alphanumeric AIS target data is automatically selected and displayed as priority. This should be treated with extreme caution and only used for enhancing situation awareness and not for collision avoidance decision-making. Such systems are also required to have the provision of selecting an alternative priority whereby the radar-tracked targets and their data, including CPA (closest point of approach) and TCPA (time to CPA), are duly displayed.

4.11 AIS will provide identification of targets together with the static and dynamic information listed in the IMO AIS Guidelines (A.1106(29)). Mariners should, however, use this information with caution noting the following important points:

4.11.1 Collision avoidance must be carried out in strict compliance with the COLREG. There is no provision in the COLREG for use of AIS information, therefore, decisions should be taken based primarily on systematic visual and/or radar observations. The availability and display of AIS data similar to one produced by systematic radar target tracking (e.g. automatic radar plotting or tracking aid (ARPA, ATA)) should not be given priority over the latter. AIS target data will only be based on the target vessels' course and speed over ground whilst for COLREG compliance such data must be based on the vessels' course and speed through the water.

4.11.2 However, the use of AIS should NOT be considered to replace the need for a visual lookout or use of "all available means" but must be used to supplement information obtained from systematic radar plotting. It is possible that if over reliance is placed on AIS information the OOW could be in breach of Rule 7(c) – "assumptions made on the basis of scanty information". Not all ships will be fitted with AIS, particularly small craft and many fishing vessels. Other floating objects which may be conspicuous on the radar will not be displayed by AIS. AIS will, however, sometimes be able to detect targets which are in a radar shadow area.

APPENDICES

4.11.3 The use of VHF to discuss actions to take between approaching ships is fraught with danger and still discouraged. MCA's view is that identification of a target by AIS does not completely alleviate the danger. Decisions on collision avoidance should be made strictly according to the COLREG.

4.11.4 AIS positions are derived from the target's EPFS receiver. This may not coincide exactly with the target as detected by radar.

4.11.5 Faulty data input to AIS could lead to incorrect or misleading information being displayed on other vessels. Mariners should remember that information derived from radar plots relies solely upon data measured by the ownship's radar and provides an accurate measurement of the target's relative course and speed, which is the most important factor in deciding upon action to avoid collision. Existing ships of less than 500GT (gross tonnage) which are not required to fit a gyro compass are unlikely to transmit heading information.

4.11.6 A recent development of AIS is the ability to provide synthetic AIS targets and virtual navigation marks as aids to navigation (AtoN), in addition to the physical AIS AtoNs, enabling coastal authorities to provide an AIS symbol on the display in any position. Mariners should bear in mind that this ability could lead to the appearance of "virtual" AIS targets and therefore take particular care when an AIS target is not complemented by a radar target. IMO guidance as in MSC.1/Circ.1473, Policy on Use of AIS Aids to Navigation, should be consulted.

5. Presentation of navigation-related symbols, terms and abbreviations

5.1 The IMO circular, issued in 2019, SN.1/Circ.243/Rev.2 'Guidelines for the presentation of navigation-related symbols, terms and abbreviations', with a view to harmonising the requirements for the presentation of navigation-related information on the bridge. These guidelines sought to ensure that all navigational displays adopt a consistent human-machine interface philosophy and implementation. These requirements come into effect from 2024/25. Until then, SN.1/Circ.243/Rev.1 Guidelines for the presentation of navigation-related symbols, terms and abbreviations, issued in 2014, should be used as the prevailing reference.

Physical AIS AtoN
Physical AIS AtoN is presented as an 'open diamond', as in Figure 1 below.

Virtual AIS AtoN
Virtual AIS AtoN is presented as an 'open diamond with crosshair centred at reported position', as in Figure 2 right:

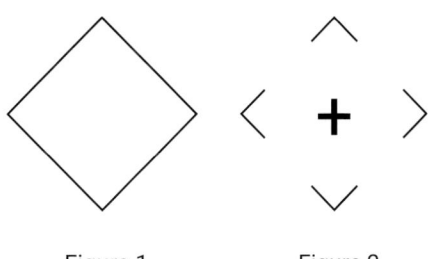

Figure 1   Figure 2

MGN 364 Amendment 1

Navigation: Traffic Separation Schemes – Application of Rule 10 and Navigation in the Dover Strait

Notice to all Shipowners, Masters, Watchkeepers, Users of TSS and all concerned with the navigation of seagoing vessels

This notice replaces and revokes Marine Guidance Note 364 (M+F)

PLEASE NOTE: Where this document provides guidance on the law it should not be regarded as definitive. The way the law applies to any particular case can vary according to circumstances - for example, from vessel to vessel and you should consider seeking independent legal advice if you are unsure of your own legal position.

Summary
- This Amendment to the MGN updates section 5 with regard to recreational activities in and around a UK traffic separation scheme (TSS).
- The International Regulations for Preventing Collisions at Sea, 1972, as amended, (COLREG), govern the conduct of all vessels in and near TSS which have been adopted by the International Maritime Organization (IMO).
- This Note draws attention to mariners on the mandatory reporting regime and the recommendations for navigating and other activities within the Dover Strait.

1. Introduction/Background

1.1 TSSs adopted by the IMO are set out in the IMO publication "Ships' Routeing", as amended, and various IMO COLREG Circulars.

1.2 Rule 10 of the COLREG, provides details for the conduct of all vessels in and near TSSs which have been adopted by IMO.

1.3 In some Schemes, special provisions may be included governing their use by specified classes of vessels. Relevant information is given on charts, or there may be a recommendation for chart users to consult Admiralty Sailing Directions for that area for details.

2. Traffic Separation Schemes – Application of Rule 10

2.1 Admiralty charts show both IMO-adopted and national authority Schemes. The current IMO publication, "Ships' Routeing", should be consulted to determine whether a particular Scheme has been adopted by the IMO.

2.2 TSSs are usually sited where there is a heavy concentration of shipping. Mariners are therefore reminded of the particular importance of strictly adhering to Rules 5, 6, 7 and 8, which refer to Look-out, Safe Speed, Risk of Collision and Action to Avoid Collision respectively.

2.3 Mariners are also reminded that except where there are special local rules to the contrary, the other Steering and Sailing Rules (Section II – Conduct of vessels in sight of one another and Section III – Conduct of vessels in restricted visibility) apply within a Scheme as they do elsewhere at sea. Vessels proceeding in a TSS do not have priority over crossing traffic.

2.4 Vessels crossing a TSS must do so on a heading as nearly as practicable at right angles to the direction of traffic flow. This minimises the time a crossing vessel is in the lane irrespective of the tidal streams and should lead to a clear encounter situation with vessels passing through the main traffic lanes.

2.5 Within the context of Rule 10(d), it is the view of the MCA that neither the density of traffic in a lane nor restricted visibility are sufficient reasons to justify the use of an Inshore Traffic Zone (ITZ), nor will the apparent absence of traffic in the ITZ qualify as a reason for not complying with this Rule.

2.6 Vessels may use an ITZ where necessary to seek shelter from weather and whilst in an ITZ, vessels may be encountered heading in any direction.

2.7 Where a TSS is bordered on both sides by an ITZ, a vessel must not use the ITZ except as permitted by Rule 10 (d).

2.8 A vessel which needs to anchor, for example because of an engine breakdown or bad visibility, may do so in a separation zone.

2.9 Vessels fishing within a Scheme are considered to be using the Scheme, and must comply with the general requirements set out in Rules 10(b) and (c), however, when fishing in a separation zone they may follow any course.

2.10 The requirement that vessels fishing must not impede the passage of traffic passing through a TSS, means that they must operate in such a manner that neither they, nor their gear, seriously restricts the sea room available to other vessels within a lane, and must take early and substantial action to avoid any risk of collision developing.

2.11 Rule 8(f) places further obligations upon fishing vessels, with regard to their responsibility not to impede the passage of any vessel following a traffic lane, and fishing vessels are not relieved from this obligation in a developing situation where risk of collision may exist. When taking any action, they must, however, take account of the possible manoeuvres of the vessel which is not to be impeded.

2.12 No specific mention is made in Rule 10(j) of a sailing vessel having an auxiliary engine, however, if such a vessel cannot follow the routeing procedures under sail because of light or adverse winds, then she should make use of her engines in order to do so, and should show the appropriate lights, shapes and sound signals for a power-driven vessel.

2.13 Maintenance of Safety of Navigation includes maintenance of navigational buoys and aids to navigation, wreck removal, hydrographic surveying and, in certain circumstances, dredging.

2.14 Many TSSs have Precautionary Areas associated with them, where traffic lanes cross or converge, so that proper separation of traffic is provided. Precautionary Areas should be avoided, if practicable, by ships not making use of the associated Schemes or deep-water routes.

2.15 Precautionary areas, although part of routeing measures, are not part of a TSS, and Rule 10 is not generally applicable, however, ships should navigate with particular caution within such areas.

2.16 Any vessel observed in a TSS which appears not to be complying with the requirements of the Scheme should be immediately notified by the best available means. If the TSS is within a Vessel Traffic Service (VTS) coverage area, the VTS should be notified.

2.17 The international two-letter signal YG meaning "you appear not to be complying with the TSS" may also be used for this purpose. The master of any vessel receiving this signal by whatever means should check their course and position and immediately take action to rectify the situation.

3. Traffic Separation Schemes – Navigation in the Dover Strait

3.1 Summary - The Dover Strait is covered by a TSS, adopted by the IMO, which is bordered by the English Inshore Traffic Zone (ITZ) and the French ITZ. The TSS and associated ITZs, the Channel Navigation Information Service (CNIS) and the Mandatory Reporting System CALDOVREP (established in accordance with SOLAS Chapter V Regulation 11) have been designed to assist seafarers to navigate these waters in safety.

3.2 TSS - Information on the TSS is provided on British Admiralty chart 5500, in the Admiralty List of Radio Signals, Volume 6(1) and in NP28, The Dover Strait Pilot. Any vessel transiting the Dover Strait must comply with the requirements of Rule 10.

3.3 ITZ - The English ITZ extends from a line drawn from the western end of the TSS to include Shoreham, to a line drawn due South from South Foreland. The French ITZ extends from Cap Gris-Nez in the north, to a line drawn due west near Le Touquet in the South.

Neither CNIS, nor HM Coastguard has the authority to grant permission for vessels to use the English ITZ in contravention of Rule 10(d). Masters deciding that circumstances warrant their use of the English ITZ, must report their decision to CNIS. Vessels may enter the ITZ if necessary to avoid immediate danger.

3.4 CNIS - Shipping movements are monitored from both Dover and Gris-Nez. Each station broadcasts information about weather and navigational hazards as part of the joint CNIS operations.

All vessels are tracked and recorded by radar and AIS – any vessel found contravening COLREG will be reported to their flag State for appropriate action to be taken. Vessels contravening collision regulations and arriving at UK ports may be liable for prosecution.

3.5 CALDOVREP - The following categories of vessels are required to participate in the Reporting System:

1. All vessels of 300GT and over;
2. All vessels of less than 300GT, should continue to report in circumstances where they:
   a. are not under command or at anchor in the TSS or an ITZ;
   b. are restricted in their ability to manoeuvre; or
   c. have defective navigational aids.

SW-bound vessels call Dover Coastguard via VHF Ch 11 not later than crossing a line drawn from North Foreland Light (51° 23'N; 001° 27'E) to the border between France and Belgium (51° 05'N; 002° 33'E).

NE-bound vessels call Gris-Nez Traffic on VHF Ch.13 when abeam the Bassurelle Light-buoy (50° 33'N; 000° 58'E).

4. Passage Planning

4.1 A passage plan and possible contingency arrangements containing all required reporting information, as well as the reporting points, should be prepared well in advance of reaching the outer limits of the reporting area. This will avoid last-minute decision-making, and searching for sources of information, enabling full concentration on traffic and navigation in the Dover Strait.

4.2 Mariners should be aware that concentration of fishing vessels and recreational craft may be encountered in the English Channel and the Dover Strait, and should navigate with caution. Fishing vessels are reminded of the requirements of Rule 10(i) and sailing vessels and other vessels of less than 20 metres in length of the requirements of Rule 10(j) of the COLREG.

4.3 Mariners are reminded that there is a concentration of crossing ferry traffic, including high speed craft, in the Dover Strait. These vessels may make course alterations outside the lanes in order to cross them at right angles. Vessels in either traffic lane may frequently have to give way to ferries and other crossing vessels in order to comply with the Steering and Sailing Rules (Rules 4 – 19) of the COLREG.

4.4 Surveillance surveys indicate that risk of collision increases if cross channel traffic, leaving Dover or the Calais approach channel, shape courses without due regard to the traffic situation in the adjacent lane. Vessels proceeding along the traffic lanes, in meeting their obligations under Rules 15 and 16, are often observed making substantial course alterations and their actions are frequently complicated when traffic converges within a particular lane.

Attention is therefore drawn to the need for cross channel traffic to take into account this possible situation arising when passage planning. Consideration should also be given to where the lane is to be crossed so that potential collision risk situations can be anticipated and are not allowed to develop. Passage planning should be dynamic and include selection and setting of a course as soon as practicable.

4.5 NE-bound vessels sailing to the Thames or UK east coast ports are required to use the NE-bound lane of the scheme where they can safely do so. A ruling on whether, in any particular case, a Master of a NE-bound vessel was justified on safety grounds in choosing to use the English ITZ rather than the NE-bound lane can only be given in a court of law.

4.6 Radar surveillance surveys show that many vessels proceeding from the NE lane towards the Thames and UK east coast ports cross the TSS in the vicinity of the MPC light-buoy. Masters are recommended to cross the SW lane in compliance with Rule 10(c) anywhere up to approximately 5 miles NE of the MPC light-buoy. In selecting the crossing point regard should be given to traffic in the SW Lane and the need to avoid the development of situations where risk of collision exists.

4.7 The F3 light-float (51° 24.'15N; 002° 00.'38E) is in an area of heavy crossing traffic. Ships leaving the West Hinder TSS and intending to transit the Dover Strait should leave the F3 on their port side, and must avoid the area within 500 metres of the light-float, when crossing the NE-bound traffic lane of the Dover Strait TSS and proceeding through the Precautionary Area.

4.8 Many vessels keep too close to the north of the SW-bound lane between South Falls and Dungeness, risking collision with the CS4 light-buoy and vessels in the English ITZ. Vessels should therefore make use of the full width of the traffic lanes and open waters to reduce collision risks. An 'area to be avoided by all vessels'; radius 3 cables, has been established around the CS4 light-buoy.

4.9 The main traffic lane for NE-bound traffic lies to the SE of the Sandettié Bank and should be followed by all such ships as can safely navigate therein having regard to their draught.

4.10 The deep-water route to the NW of the Sandettié Bank is intended for use by vessels with a draught of 16 metres or more. Masters considering using this route should take into account the proximity of traffic using the SW-bound lane. Through traffic to which this consideration does not apply should, if practicable, avoid using the deep-water route.

4.11 In two-way routes, including two-way deep-water routes, vessels should, as far as practicable, keep to the starboard side of the marked route. Vessels using deep-water routes are recommended to avoid overtaking.

4.12 Master of ships, when planning their passage through the Dover Strait and its approaches, should ensure that there is an adequate under-keel clearance at the time of passage. To achieve this, allowance must be made for the effects of squat at the passage speed, for uncertainties in charted depths and tide levels, and for the effects of waves and swell resulting from local and distant storms.

4.13 In assessing a safe under-keel allowance, masters of vessels constrained by their draught are strongly advised to consult the Sailing Directions, Mariners' Routeing Guides and Deep-Draught Planning Guides published for the area by hydrographic offices, and to be guided by the recommendations for under-keel allowance contained therein.

APPENDICES

4.14 When calculating the depth of water, mariners are reminded that the height of the tide in mid-Strait can be up to one metre less than predicted for the adjacent standard port.

4.15 Special consideration during passage planning should be given to passing the Varne bank and associated shallow waters, which is located centrally within the SW lane and marked by cardinal buoys and a lightship at its northern end. Vessels transiting the SW lane are permitted to pass either side of the Varne Bank.

Tugs and tows with long towline arrangements

4.16 Tug and tow arrangements, especially with long tows, need to exercise particular care through busy traffic areas such as the Dover Strait. To ensure safe transit, in addition to the correct COLREG lights and shapes, it is considered best practice to:
1. pass through the most critical areas during daylight;
2. have a guard vessel marking the end of the tow and/or patrolling length of the tow;
3. do a WZ (coastal warning) promulgation, particularly with long tows when the length exceeds 500m;
4. report early to Dover Coastguard on approach to the CALDOVREP reporting area; and
5. keeping Dover Coastguard informed of the tug and tow approach and passage throughout transit.

5. Recreational Activities in a UK TSS

5.1 Recreational diving within a UK TSS, is not recommended as it presents a hazard to the safety of navigation. Vessels must always proceed in the general direction of traffic flow for that lane. They should not impede the safe passage of a power-driven vessel following a traffic lane, nor should they anchor in the lane.

5.2 Recreational divers considering participating in diving in any TSS, are reminded that deep draught and high-speed ships transiting TSSs may be unable to detect typical diving surface marker buoys at distance. Some vessels may also have a draught in excess of 10 metres, which may pose additional problems for divers contemplating decompression stops above that depth. Such vessels also generate wash and wake that may create difficulties when recovering divers from the water, or for dive support craft with low freeboards.

5.3 Masters of dive support craft in the Dover Strait should always advise CNIS, of their intentions in order to promote diving safety, and to benefit from any safety advice that may be available.

5.4 Mariners should be aware that during summer months (April–September) through traffic may encounter channel crossings by swimmers or other unorthodox craft. These will normally be attended by support vessels fitted with AIS and complying with the COLREG. Information regarding these crossings is routinely broadcast by CNIS.

MGN 369 (M+F)

Navigation: Navigation In Restricted Visibility
Notice to all Ship Owners, Masters, Skippers, Ships' Officers, and Pilots.
This notice replaces Marine Guidance Note 202 and should be read in conjunction with MGN 313 Keeping a Safe Navigational Watch on Fishing Vessels and MGN 315 Keeping a Safe Navigational Watch on Merchant Vessels.

PLEASE NOTE:
Where this document provides guidance on the law it should not be regarded as definitive. The way the law applies to any particular case can vary according to circumstances - for example, from vessel to vessel and you should consider seeking independent legal advice if you are unsure of your own legal position.

MARINE GUIDANCE NOTE

Summary

A 2003 survey published by the Nautical Institute (Seaways–Roger Syms) showed that many Officers of the Watch (OOW) do not fully understand and properly follow the International Regulations for the Prevention of Collisions at Sea (COLREGS) and as a consequence collisions still occur.

This Guidance note;
- Describes the proper conduct of vessels in restricted visibility
- Sets out how to apply the Rule to determine risk of collision in a close-quarters situation and decide on the correct avoiding action
- Reminds operators that Sections I and III of the Steering and Sailing Rules of the Collision Regulations must be complied with strictly
- Advises operators on how they should determine a safe speed and a close-quarters situation in restricted visibility.

Key Points
- Navigating a ship in restricted visibility requires a full understanding of the COLREGS, in particular Part B (Steering and Sailing Rules) both Section III (Rule 19) – Conduct of vessels in restricted visibility and Section I (Rules 4 to 10 inclusive) – Conduct of vessels in any condition of visibility.
- It is the responsibility of the OOW to comply with the COLREGS. Companies have to ensure compliance of their employees with COLREGS and issue guidance to that extent but the ultimate decision about safe navigation has to be made by the OOW taking into account all available information.

APPENDICES

- Rule 19 is the basis for navigation in reduced visibility; this Rule requires that a vessel shall proceed at a safe speed adapted to the prevailing circumstances, initially to be judged by all factors listed in Rule 6. Rule 19 requires that there is no stand-on vessel. All participants are required to take appropriate avoiding action.
- Keeping a proper look-out requires the OOW to ensure that all available means are used to obtain as much information as possible about the current traffic and navigation situation and then evaluate this information before taking action.

1. Introduction
1.1 This Marine Guidance Notice (MGN) explains the Maritime and Coastguard Agency (MCA) understanding of terms such as 'forward of the beam', 'safe speed', 'close-quarters situation', 'closest point of approach' (CPA), 'risk of collision' and 'proper look-out'.
1.2 This guidance does not free any company, Master and/or Officer of the Watch (OOW) of their responsibility to take decisions about the safe operation of their ship in accordance with the law.
1.3 Many sources have been used as a basis for this MGN including MAIB collision investigation reports, The International Chamber of Shipping Bridge Procedures Guide, The Standards for Training and Certification for Watch Keepers 1978, as amended, North of England Protection and Indemnity Club (P&I), UK Admiralty Court and Court of Appeal judgements.

2. Rule 1 – Application
(a) These Rules shall apply to all vessels upon the high seas and in all waters connected therewith navigable by seagoing vessels.

3. Steering and Sailing Rules
3.1 Part B of the COLREGS has three sections:
Section I (Rules 4–10) Conduct of vessels in any condition of visibility. Section II (Rules 11–18) Conduct of vessels in sight of one another and Section III (Rule 19) Conduct of vessels not in sight of one another.

4. Rule 19 – Conduct of vessels in restricted visibility
(a) This Rule applies to vessels not in sight of one another when navigating in or near an area of restricted visibility.
- If you cannot see the other vessel visually, then Rule 19 shall apply, regardless of whether your vessel is in or near an area of restricted visibility

(b) Every vessel shall proceed at a safe speed adapted to the prevailing circumstances and conditions of restricted visibility. A power-driven vessel shall have her engines ready for immediate manoeuvre.

- Safe speed cannot be explained in absolute numbers for all vessels
- The factors that determine a safe speed are dealt with in detail by Rule 6
- Strong winds and high seas may influence the manoeuvrability of the vessel
- Determination of safe speed must be continuously re-assessed as circumstances change
- The OOW should be aware of the effect that different load conditions (full or partly loaded or in ballast) will have on the vessel handling characteristics

(c) Every vessel shall have due regard to the prevailing circumstances and conditions of restricted visibility when complying with the Rules of Section I of this Part.
- When navigating in or near areas of restricted visibility Rule 19 is not the only Rule from Part B (Steering and Sailing Rules) that applies, Rules 4 to 10 inclusive (of Section I), also apply

(d) A vessel which detects by radar alone the presence of another vessel shall determine if a close-quarters situation is developing and/or risk of collision exists. If so, she shall take avoiding action in ample time, provided that when such action consists of an alteration of course, so far as possible the following shall be avoided:
  (i) an alteration of course to port for a vessel forward of the beam, other than for a vessel being overtaken;
  (ii) an alteration of course towards a vessel abeam or abaft the beam.
- If risk of collision or a close-quarters situation is developing then avoiding action must be taken because there are no stand-on vessels under Rule 19
- If the target posing the risk of collision or a close-quarters situation is forward of your beam: Try to avoid altering to port for that vessel, unless you are overtaking it
- If the target posing the risk of collision or a close-quarters situation is abeam or abaft of your beam: Try to avoid altering course in a direction that would take you towards that vessel

(e) Except where it has been determined that a risk of collision does not exist, every vessel which hears apparently forward of her beam the fog signal of another vessel, or which cannot avoid a close-quarters situation with another vessel forward of her beam, shall reduce her speed to the minimum at which she can be kept on her course. She shall if necessary take all her way off and in any event navigate with extreme caution until danger of collision is over.
- Keep an effective listening watch for fog signals
- Have the engines ready for immediate manoeuvre
- Reducing speed may allow more time to assess the situation
- Not all vessels will be detected by radar, specially yachts and other small craft

APPENDICES

- If a fog signal is heard it may be difficult to accurately determine the direction of the fog signal

5. Rule 5 – Look-out
Every vessel shall at all times maintain a proper look-out by sight and hearing as well as by all available means appropriate in the prevailing circumstances and conditions so as to make a full appraisal of the situation and of the risk of collision.
- Maintaining a proper Look-out is an important element of safe watchkeeping, especially when the visibility is restricted, and includes look-out by hearing, radar, VHF, AIS as well as by sight.

6. Rule 6 – Safe Speed
6.1 Rule 6 states that, every vessel shall at all times proceed at a safe speed so that she can take proper and effective action to avoid collision and be stopped within a distance appropriate to the prevailing circumstances and conditions. Rule 6(a) lists the factors for safe speed that apply to all vessels, and Rule 6(b) lists factors that apply to ships fitted with radar.

6.2 Rule 19 reinforces Rule 6 by requiring all vessels to proceed at a safe speed in restricted visibility and by requiring power-driven vessels to 'have their engines ready for immediate manoeuvre'.

6.3 In order to maintain a safe speed at all times a continuous appraisal of changes in circumstances and conditions should be made.

7. Rule 7 – Risk of Collision
(a) Every vessel shall use all available means appropriate to the prevailing circumstances and conditions to determine if risk of collision exists. If there is any doubt such risk shall be deemed to exist.
- Use radar for assessing the risk of collision
- Maintain a good visual and listening watch at all times
- If in doubt, assume that risk of collision exists and act accordingly

(b) Proper use shall be made of radar equipment if fitted and operational, including long-range scanning to obtain early warning of risk of collision and radar plotting or equivalent systematic observation of detected objects.
- ARPA only produces systematic observation of acquired targets
- Make sure radar and ARPA are used to their full potential. They should be properly aligned and adjusted
- Make systematic observations of targets to assess risk of collision and build up situation awareness
- Use radar range-scale properly; that is, use shorter ranges when dealing with

targets closer to your vessel and long-range scanning to provide early warning
- An operational radar is one without defects. All functions of the equipment have to be available for the operator and there should be no loss of target brilliance due to a worn out cathode ray tube or missing pixels of the liquid crystal display monitor. Particularly loss of targets near the centre, including clutter, would be an obvious concern

(c) Assumptions shall not be made on the basis of scanty information, especially scanty radar information.
- Take time to assess every situation properly, as it requires several minutes of systematic observation to produce useful information from a radar or ARPA set

(d) In determining if risk of collision exists the following considerations shall be among those taken into account
  (i) Such risks shall be deemed to exist if the compass bearing of an approaching vessel does not appreciably change
  (ii) Such risk may sometimes exist even when an appreciable bearing change is evident, particularly when approaching a very large vessel or a tow or when approaching a vessel at close range
- Determine risk of collision from a systematic plotting of targets
- Risk of collision exists if the compass bearing does not appreciably change
- Relative motion trails on a radar provide a reliable indication of collision risk
- Observing the compass bearing of a target is one means of determining whether risk of collision exists
- In restricted visibility the only way to observe the compass bearing of a target is to use a compass-stabilised radar
- Even if the compass bearing does appreciably change, there may still be a risk of collision when approaching large targets or when approaching targets at close range
- An electronic bearing line (EBL) fixed to own-ship is a convenient way of observing changes to the compass bearing of a target
- On an ARPA display, risk of collision with a tracked target exists if the relative vector of the target points at own-ships' position on the screen
- CPA & TCPA alarms can be set to provide warning of collision risk or potential close quarters situation with tracked targets

8. Rule 8– Action to Avoid Collision
(a) Any action to avoid collision shall be taken in accordance with the Rules of this part and shall, if the circumstances of the case admit, be positive, made in ample time and with due regard to the observance of good seamanship.
- Observe good seamanship
- Comply with the steering and sailing Rules

- Take early action which results in a safe outcome

(b) Any alteration of course and/or speed to avoid collision shall, if the circumstances of the case admit, be large enough to be readily apparent to another vessel observing visually or by radar; a succession of small alterations of course and/or speed should be avoided.
- Do not make a series of small alterations
- Alterations should be readily apparent to other vessels
- Course alterations tend to be more readily apparent than change in speed

(c) If there is sufficient sea-room, alteration of course alone may be the most effective action to avoid a close-quarters situation provided that it is made in good time, is substantial and does not result in another close-quarters situation.

(d) Action taken to avoid collision with another vessel shall be such as to result in passing at a safe distance. The effectiveness of the action shall be carefully checked until the other vessel is finally past and clear.
- Keep a safe distance from other vessels
- It is important to systematically observe the effectiveness of the action taken
- The safe distance will depend on the circumstances, however if you have sufficient sea room there is no reason to pass close to another vessel

(e) If necessary to avoid collision or allow more time to assess the situation, a vessel shall slacken her speed or take all way off by stopping or reversing her means of propulsion.
- A power-driven vessel should have the engines ready for immediate manoeuvre

(f) "A vessel which, by any of these Rules, is required not to impede the passage or safe passage of another vessel"…etc.
- The requirement not to impede the passage or safe passage of another vessel does not apply only to vessels in sight of each other which are approaching in such a way that risk of collision is likely to develop.
- The requirements of Rule 8(f) together with Rules 9(b), (c) and (d), and 10(i) and (j) apply in both clear and restricted visibility.
- When there is an obligation not to impede in restricted visibility Rule 19 applies fully, together with Rule 8(f)

9. Forward of the Beam
9.1 A vessel is forward of the beam as long as her relative bearing from the observing vessel is less than 90° or more than 270°.

10. Close-quarters Situation
10.1 Similar to 'safe speed' a 'close-quarters situation' depends on the particular

circumstances and closing speeds of the vessels involved. Manoeuvring characteristics, visibility, weather, traffic density, restricted or open waters, will all have an influence on determining at what distance a close-quarters situation begins to exist. A close-quarters situation is not to be confused with a risk of collision which begins at an earlier point in time.

11. Closest Point of Approach (CPA)

11.1 Systematic observation of a radar target offers a forecast of the distance off at which a target will pass (the closest point of approach or CPA) and the time at which the target will reach its closest point of approach (TCPA). This information is an effective measure of the risk of close-quarters situation developing.

11.2 The ARPA or ATA must track the target(s) for a period of time, after which a vector can be displayed. Using the vector length control, the vectors can be extended to determine the CPA by observation against the back ground of the range rings and the TCPA can be read off from the vector length control.

11.3 It is possible to specify a CPA and TCPA (sometimes referred to as safe limits) which will activate an alarm if both are violated. For example, if the CPA and TCPA controls are set to 0.5 n miles and 30 min respectively and a target which is being tracked will come to a CPA of less than 0.5 n miles in less than 30 min, then the alarm will be activated.

12. MAIB Reported Collision Cases

12.1 A number of collisions in restricted visibility over the past years demonstrated that some of the vessels involved were neither well run nor was sufficient competency, awareness and conscientiousness displayed by bridge crews and skippers of vessels involved. *(See the following MAIB investigation reports: Diamont/Northern Merchant (2002), P&O Nedlloyd Vespucci/Wahkuna (2003), Lykes Voyager/Washington Senator (2006)).*

12.2 In 2002 a collision investigated by the MAIB involving a high-speed craft (HSC) and a ro-ro ferry on a crossing course in the Dover Strait, indicated the HSC was making 32 knots and the ro-ro ferry was making 21 knots. The predicted CPA was 3 cables.

12.3 The 2003 collision happened in the middle of the English Channel north of Cherbourg between a container ship making 25 knots on a crossing course with a sailing yacht making 7.5 knots. The predicted CPA was 8 cables.

12.4 The 2006 case involved two container vessels just north of the Taiwan Banks, on crossing courses with one making 17 knots and the other 19.5 knots. The predicted CPA was 2-3 cables.

12.5 Some of the key contributing factors identified in the above three collisions were excessive speed and too small a CPA. This is in line with findings of a wider study according to which approximately 60% of all collisions are said to involve excessive speed.

12.6 Rule 19(b) requires that all ships shall proceed at a safe speed, and in case of power-driven vessels shall also have their engines ready for immediate manoeuvre.

13. Commercial Considerations

13.1 Speed of a ship and thereby fuel consumption and the related costs are usually dictated by commercial interests. Even though a company has the right to give instructions to masters these instructions cannot overrule their decision on safety matters. Particular reference is made to the Regulation 34-1 "Master's Discretion" of SOLAS Chapter V.

"The owner, the charterer, the company operating the ship as defined in regulation IX/1, or any other person shall not prevent or restrict the Master of the ship from taking or executing any decision which, in the Master's professional judgement, is necessary for safety of life at sea and protection of the marine environment."

The MCA interpret this as ensuring the Master has absolute discretion to take decisions in the interests of safety of life at sea and or protection of the marine environment.

13.2 Companies are advised to stress this point in their Safety Management System and positively encourage Masters and OOWs to follow safe navigational practices in any situation, particularly in restricted visibility. Positive encouragement may be required to make the master and officers fully aware that it may be of disadvantage to the company for bridge teams not to comply with rules and regulations and the COLREGS in particular.

14. Well Run Ship

14.1 A 'well run ship' will under all circumstances be navigated in accordance with the regulations. This does not only require the OOW to follow the COLREGS but also obligates the company to provide the necessary resources and issue relevant guidance in compliance with the International Safety Management (ISM) Code.

14.2 Good Bridge Team Management is an essential tool in ensuring that a ship is well run. Navigators should be familiar with the contents of the latest International Chamber of Shipping (ICS) Bridge Procedures Guide.

15. Conclusion

In conditions of restricted visibility when complying with Rule 19; there are no stand-on or give-way vessels. All vessels are required to determine whether a close-quarters situation is developing and if a risk of collision exists. If the likelihood of a close-quarters situation is detected then each vessel must take appropriate action to prevent the close-quarters situation from developing.

The judgment as to when a vessel is heading in to a close-quarters situation will have to be made by individual OOWs using all available means combined with their own experience and good seamanship. Over reliance must not be placed on calculated CPAs and TCPAs from ARPA equipment. Navigational constraints, environmental factors and knowledge of own vessels manoeuvrability must also be taken into account when reaching this judgement.

OOWs should be encouraged to call the Master, or seek the view of more experienced members of the bridge team in ample time to assist in assessing the situation.

Annex

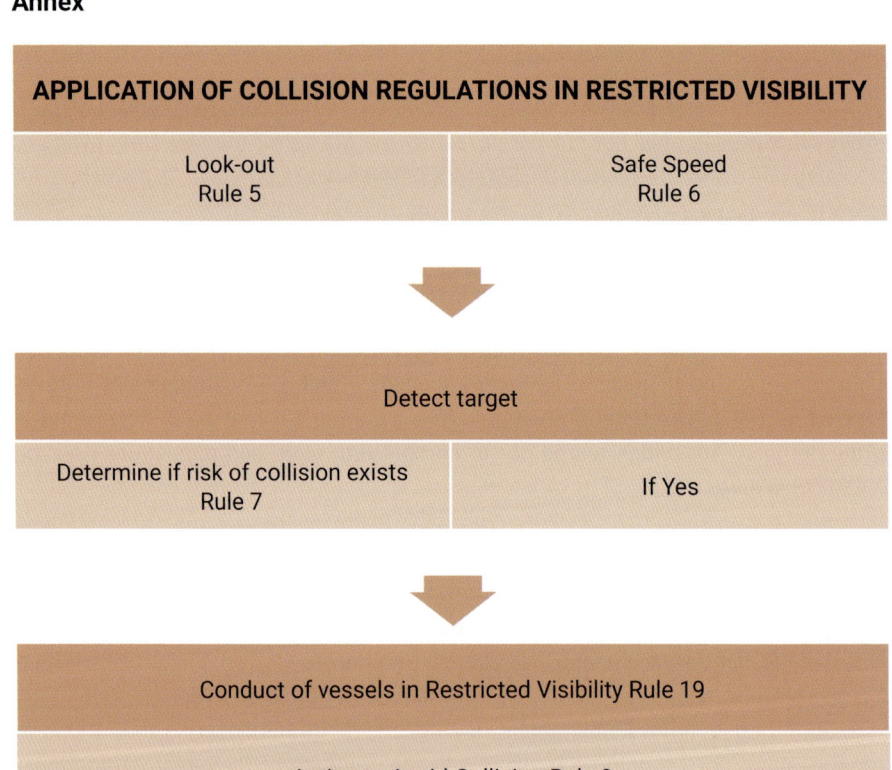

MGN 379 (M+F)

Navigation: Use of Electronic Navigation Aids
Notice to all Owners, Masters, Skippers, Officers and Crews of Merchant Ships and Fishing Vessels.
This notice replaces MGN 63

PLEASE NOTE:
Where this document provides guidance on the law it should not be regarded as definitive. The way the law applies to any particular case can vary according to circumstances - for example, from vessel to vessel and you should consider seeking independent legal advice if you are unsure of your own legal position.

MARINE GUIDANCE NOTE

Summary
This note emphasises the need for correct use of navigational equipment by watch-keepers.

Key Points
- Be aware that each item of equipment is an aid to navigation.
- Be aware of the factors which affect the accuracy of position fixing systems.
- Appreciate the need to cross check position fixing information using other methods.
- Recognise the importance of the correct use of navigational aids and knowledge of their limitations.
- Be aware of the dangers of over-reliance on the output from, and accuracy of, a single navigational aid.

1. Introduction
Accidents have occurred where the primary cause has been over-reliance on a single electronic navigational aid. Watch-keepers must always ensure that positional information is regularly cross-checked using other equipment, as well as visual aids to navigation. In other cases accidents have occurred where the watch-keeper was not fully conversant with the operation of equipment or its limitations.

2. Provision of Navigational Equipment on Ships
The Merchant Shipping (Safety of Navigation) Regulations 2002 (SI 2002 No 1473) implement the carriage requirements for navigational equipment set out in Regulation 19 of Safety of Life at Sea (SOLAS) Chapter V. These requirements, together with guidance notes, are contained in the 2007 Edition of the Maritime and Coastguard

Agency (MCA) publication "Safety of Navigation – Implementing SOLAS Chapter V 2002"

Ships built before 1 July 2002 may continue to comply with the requirements of SOLAS Chapter V/74 in force prior to 2002 Regulations, with regard to Signalling Lamps (Reg. 11/74), Navigation Equipment (Reg. 12/74) and Nautical Publications (Reg. 20/74). However they must carry a Global Navigation Satellite System (GNSS) receiver or a terrestrial radionavigation receiver, Automatic Identification System (AIS) and Voyage Data Recorder (VDR) or Simplified Voyage Data Recorder (S-VDR) in accordance with the timetables set out in Regulations 19 and 20 of SOLAS V 2002.

Guidance is also given in Annex 20 of the MCA Safety of Navigation publication on siting and servicing of the installations.

3. Radar and Plotting Aids
3.1 General
Collisions have been frequently caused by failure to make proper use of radar and radar plotting aids in both restricted visibility and clear weather. Common errors have been deciding to alter course on the basis of insufficient information and maintaining too high a speed, particularly when a close-quarters situation is developing. Information provided by radar and radar plotting aids in clear weather conditions can assist the watch-keeper in maintaining a proper lookout in areas of high traffic density. It is most important to remember that navigation in restricted visibility can be more demanding and great care is needed even with all the information available from the radar and radar plotting aids. Where continuous radar watch-keeping and plotting cannot be maintained even greater caution must be exercised. A "safe speed" should at all times reflect the prevailing circumstances.

3.2 Electronic radar plotting aids
Radars must be equipped with plotting aids, the type of which depends upon the size of ship as follows;

a) Electronic Plotting Aid (EPA)
EPA equipment enables electronic plotting of at least 10 targets, but without automatic tracking (Ships between 300 and 500 Gross Tonnage (GT)).

b) Automatic Tracking Aid (ATA)
ATA equipment enables manual acquisition and automatic tracking and display of at least 10 targets (Ships over 500 GT).

On ships of 3000 GT and over the second radar must also be equipped with an ATA, the two ATAs must be functionally independent of each other.

c) Automatic Radar Plotting Aid (ARPA)
ARPA equipment provides for manual or automatic acquisition of targets and the automatic tracking and display of all relevant target information for at least 20 targets for anti-collision decision making. It also enables trial manoeuvre to be executed (Ships of 10000 GT and over).

The second radar must incorporate ATA if not ARPA.

Manual plotting equipment is no longer acceptable except for existing vessels still complying with SOLAS V/74.

Watch-keepers must be fully conversant with the operation and limitations of these plotting facilities and should practice using them in clear-weather conditions to improve their skills.

In addition to the advice given above and the instructions contained in the Operating Manual(s), users of radar plotting aids should ensure that:

(i) performance of the radar is monitored and optimised

(ii) test programmes provided are used to check the validity of the plotting data, and

(iii) speed and heading inputs to the ARPA/ATA are satisfactory. Correct speed input, where provided by manual setting of the appropriate ARPA/ATA controls or by an external input, is vital for correct processing of ARPA/ATA data. Serious errors in output data can arise if heading and/or speed inputs to the ARPA/ATA are incorrect.

For full details of the carriage requirements and associated guidance see Regulation 19 and Annex 16 of the MCA Safety of Navigation publication.

3.3 Plotting

To estimate risk of collision with another vessel the closest point of approach (CPA) must be established. Choice of appropriate avoiding action is facilitated by the knowledge of the other vessel's track using the manual or automatic plotting methods (see 3.2 above). The accuracy of the plot, however obtained, depends upon accurate measurement of own ship's track during the plotting interval. It is important to note that an inaccurate compass heading or speed input will reduce the accuracy of true vectors when using ARPA or ATA. This is particularly important with targets on near-reciprocal courses where a slight error in own-ship's data may lead to a dangerous interpretation of the target vessel's true track. The apparent precision of digital read-outs should be treated with caution.

If two radars are fitted (mandatory for ships of 3000 GT and over) it is good practice, especially in restricted visibility or in congested waters, for one to be designated for anti-collision work, while the other is used to assist navigation. If only one of the radars is fitted with ARPA then this should be the one used for anti-collision work and the other for navigation.

3.4 Interpretation

It is essential for the operator to be aware of the radar's current performance which is best ascertained by the Performance Monitor. The echo return from a distant known target should also be checked. Be aware of the possibility that small vessels, ice floes or other floating objects such as containers may not be detected.

Echoes may be obscured by sea- or rain-clutter. Correct setting of clutter controls will help but may not completely remove this possibility. When plotting larger targets on a medium-range scale, the display should be periodically switched to a shorter range, and the clutter controls adjusted, to search for less distinct targets.

The observer must be aware of the arcs of blind and shadow sectors on the display caused by masts and other on-board obstructions. These sectors must be plotted on a diagram placed near the radar display. This diagram must be updated following any changes which affect the sectors.

3.5 Choice of range scale

Although the choice of range scales for observation and plotting is dependent upon several factors such as traffic density, speed of own-ship and the frequency of observation, it is not generally advisable to commence plotting on a short-range scale. Advance warning of the approach of other vessels, changes in traffic density, or proximity of the coastline, should be obtained by occasional use of longer-range scales. This applies particularly when approaching areas where high traffic density is likely, when information obtained from the use of longer-range scales may be an important factor in determining a safe speed.

3.6 Appreciation

A single observation of the range and bearing of an echo will give no indication of the track of a vessel in relation to own ship. To estimate this, a succession of observations must be made over a known time interval. The longer the period of observation, the more accurate the result will be. This also applies to ARPA/ATA which requires adequate time to produce accurate information suitable for assessing CPA/TCPA and determining appropriate manoeuvres.

Estimation of the target's true track is only valid up to the time of the last observation and the situation must be kept constantly under review. The other vessel, which may not be keeping a radar watch or plotting, may subsequently alter its course and/or speed. This will take time to become apparent to the observer. Electronic plotting will not detect any alteration of a target's course or speed immediately and therefore should also be monitored constantly.

The compass bearing, either visual or radar should be used to assess risk of collision. The relative bearing of a target should not be used when own-ship's course and/or speed alters, as risk of collision may still exist even where the relative bearing is changing. Mariners should also be aware that at close range, risk of collision may exist even with a changing compass bearing.

Radar displays may be equipped to display AIS target data. Such information may be used to assist the observer in assessing the situation and taking correct action to avoid a close-quarters situation. Watch-keepers should be aware that not all vessels transmit AIS data. In addition it is possible that not all the AIS data displayed will be accurate, particularly data which is inputted manually on the target vessel.

3.7 Clear weather practice

Radar should be used to complement visual observations in clear weather to assist assessment of whether risk of collision exists or is likely to develop. Radar provides accurate determination of range enabling appropriate action to be taken in sufficient time to avoid collision, taking into account the manoeuvring capabilities of own ship.

It is important that watch-keepers should regularly practice using radar and the electronic plotting system in clear weather. This allows radar observations and the resulting electronic vectors to be checked visually. It will show up any misinterpretation of the radar display or misleading appraisal of the situation, which could be dangerous in restricted visibility. By keeping themselves familiar with the process of systematic radar observations, and comparing the relationship between radar and electronically plotted information and the actual situation, watchkeepers will be able to deal rapidly and competently with the problems which may confront them in restricted visibility.

3.8 Operation

Radar if fitted should be operating at all times. When weather conditions indicate that visibility may deteriorate, and at night when small craft or unlit obstructions such as ice are likely to be encountered, both radars if fitted should be operating, with one dedicated to anti-collision work. This is particularly important when there is a likelihood of occasional fog banks, so that vessels can be detected before entering the fog. Radars are designed for continuous operation and frequently switching them on and off could damage components.

3.9 Parallel Index technique

Investigations into cases where vessels have run aground have often shown that, when radar was being used as an aid to navigation, inadequate monitoring of the ship's position was a contributory factor.

Parallel Index techniques provide the means of continuously monitoring a vessel's position in relation to a pre-determined passage plan, and would in some cases have helped to avoid these groundings. Parallel indexing should be practised in clear weather during straightforward passages, so that watch-keepers remain thoroughly familiar with the technique and confident in its use in more demanding situations (in confined waters, restricted visibility or at night).

The principles of Parallel Index plotting can be applied, using electronic index lines. A number of index lines may be pre-set and called up when required on all modes of display: electronic index lines remain at the set cross index range (CIR) enabling the operator to change range without corrupting the range of the index line. Care should be exercised when activating preset parallel index lines that the correct line(s) for the passage are being displayed.

a) Parallel indexing on a relative motion display

On a relative motion compass-stabilised radar display, the echo of a fixed object will move across the display in a direction and at a speed which is the exact reciprocal of own ship's ground track: parallel indexing uses this principle of relative motion. Reference is first made to the chart and the planned ground track. The index line is drawn parallel to the planned ground track at a perpendicular distance (cross index range or offset) equal to the planned passing distance off an appropriate fixed target. Observation of the fixed object's echo movement along the index line will indicate whether the ship is maintaining the planned track: any displacement of the echo from the index line will immediately indicate that own ship is not maintaining the desired ground track, enabling corrective action to be taken.

b) Parallel indexing on a true motion display

The use of a true motion radar presentation for parallel indexing requires an ability to ground-stabilise the display reliably. Parallel index lines are fixed relative to the trace origin (i.e. to own ship), and consequently move across the display at the same rate and in the same direction as own ship. Being drawn parallel to the planned charted track and offset at the required passing distance off the selected fixed mark, the echo of the mark will move along the index line as long as the ship remains on track. Any displacement of the fixed mark's echo from the index line will indicate that the ship is off track, enabling corrective action to be taken.

c) Integration with ECDIS

Where the radar display is integrated with an Electronic Chart Display and Information System (ECDIS) the practice of parallel indexing continues to enable the navigator to monitor the ship's position relative to the planned track and additionally provides a means of continuously monitoring the positional integrity of the ECDIS system.

d) Precautions

Some older radars may still have reflection plotters. It is important to remember that parallel index lines drawn on reflection plotters apply to one range scale only. In addition to all other precautions necessary for the safe use of radar information, particular care must therefore be taken when changing range scales.

The use of parallel indexing does not remove the requirement for position fixing at regular intervals using all appropriate methods available including visual bearings, since parallel indexing only indicates if the ship is on or off track and not its progress along the track.

When using radar for position fixing and monitoring, check:

(i) the identity of fixed objects,
(ii) the radar's overall performance,
(iii) the gyro error and accuracy of the heading marker alignment,
(iv) that parallel index lines are correctly positioned on a suitable display, and
(v) the accuracy of the variable range marker, bearing cursor and fixed range rings.

3.10 Chart Radar
Some radars are provided with electronic chart overlays. These charts may have a limited amount of data and are not the equivalent to an Electronic Navigational Chart (ENC) used in the ECDIS or paper charts. They should not therefore be used as the primary basis for navigation.

3.11 Regular operational checks
Frequent checks of the radar performance must be made to ensure that the quality of the display has not deteriorated.

The performance of the radar should be checked using the Performance Monitor before sailing and at least every four hours whilst a radar watch is being maintained.

Misalignment of the heading marker, even if only slightly, can lead to dangerously misleading interpretation of potential collision situations, particularly in restricted visibility when targets are approaching from ahead or fine on own ship's bow. It is therefore important that checks of the heading marker should be made periodically to ensure that correct alignment is maintained. If misalignment exists it should be corrected at the earliest opportunity. The following procedures are recommended:

a) Check that the heading marker is aligned with the true compass heading of the ship.
b) Ensure that the heading marker line on the display is aligned with the fore-and-aft line of the ship. This is done by selecting a conspicuous but small object with a small and distinct echo which is clearly identifiable and lies as near as possible at the edge of the range scale in use. Measure simultaneously the relative visual bearing of this object and the relative bearing on the display. Any misalignment must be removed in accordance with the instructions in the equipment manual.

To avoid introducing serious bearing errors, adjustment of the heading marker should not be carried out:
  (i) when alongside a berth by using the berth's alignment.
  (ii) using bearings of targets which are close to the vessel, not distinct or have not been identified with certainty both by radar and visually.

3.12 Stabilisation modes
It is important to select the optimum stabilisation mode for the radar display. To assess risk of collision the relative motion of a target gives the clearest indication of CPA and may be monitored by observing either the direction of the target's relative trail, or the CPA predicted by the relative vector.

By default, relative motion will display relative target trails and true motion will display true target trails.

Where true target trails is selected, a sea-stabilised display will indicate all targets' motion through the water. A ground-stabilised display will indicate all targets' motion over the ground.

In coastal, estuarial and river waters where a significant set and drift may be experienced, a sea-stabilised display will produce significant target trails from all fixed (stationary) objects possibly producing an unacceptably high level of clutter and masking. In such circumstances a ground-stabilised display may reduce its effect and enable the observer to detect clearly the trails of moving targets, thus enhancing the observer's situational awareness.

It should be noted that the observed and predicted relative motion of a target is unaffected by the choice of sea or ground stabilisation, allowing the same assessment of CPA and risk of collision. If switching between sea and ground stabilisation, the observer should be aware of the time required for the radar equipment to reprocess the stabilisation input data.

3.13 Speed Input

It should be noted that in determining a target's aspect by radar; the calculation of its true track is dependent on the choice and accuracy of the own ship's course and speed input. A ground-stabilised target plot may accurately calculate the ground track of the target, but its heading may be significantly different from its track when experiencing set, drift or leeway. Similarly, a sea-stabilised target plot may be inaccurate when own ship and the target, are experiencing different rates of set, drift or leeway.

3.14 Gyro failure

In cases of gyro failure when the radar's heading data is provided from a transmitting magnetic heading device (TMHD), watch-keepers should determine and apply the magnetic compass errors.

The true vector function of automatic plotting and tracking equipment should be operated with caution when the heading input is derived from a Transmitting Magnetic Compass (TMC). ARPA prediction is reliant on steady state tracking, where course and speed remain steady: In a seaway a transmitting magnetic compass may not produce a sufficiently steady heading resulting in unreliable vectors.

3.15 Warnings and alarms

Audible operational warnings and alarms may be used to indicate that a target has closed on a pre-set range, enters a user-selected guard zone or violates a preset CPA or TCPA limit.

When the ARPA is in automatic acquisition mode, these alarms should be used with caution, especially in the vicinity of small radar-inconspicuous targets. Users should familiarise themselves with the effects of error sources on the automatic tracking of targets by reference to the ARPA Operating Manual. Such alarms do not relieve the user from the duty to maintain a proper lookout by all available means.

3.16 SARTS and other Radar Transponders

Information on detection and use of Search and Rescue Transponders (SARTs) is provided in Chapter 4 of Volume 5 of the Admiralty List of Radio Signals. Watch-keepers should note that 3 GHz ("S" Band) radars will not detect SARTS or other radar transponders, such as small-craft radar enhancers, as these transmit only in the 9 GHz ("X" Band) frequency.

APPENDICES

4. Electronic Positioning Systems

4.1 General

Ships are required to carry a Global Navigation Satellite System (GNSS) receiver or a terrestrial radio-navigation receiver. While both Omega and Decca have already been discontinued, LORAN C is to be retained for the time being but does not give world-wide coverage. Within its chain coverage area LORAN provides maritime users with a terrestrial system to back-up GNSS in the event of that system's failure.

4.2 LORAN C

LORAN C is based on the measurement of time difference between the reception of transmitted pulses. The ground-wave coverage is typically between 800 and 1200 miles, although the accuracy of positional information will depend upon the relative position of the transmitters. LORAN coverage is limited to North America, Europe, the Middle East, SE Asia and parts of the Pacific Rim.

When entering the coverage, or when passing close to transmitters on the coast, the receiver may have difficulty in identifying the correct ground-wave cycle to track. Under these conditions care should be taken to cross-check the positions obtained from the LORAN C receiver with positions from other position-fixing systems to ensure that it is tracking on the correct cycle.

The fixed errors of the LORAN C system are caused by variations in the velocity at which the pulses travel. Additional Secondary Factor (ASF) corrections are provided to allow for these errors which may be very significant in some areas. Some receivers automatically allow for calculated ASF values and display a corrected position.

4.3 Enhanced LORAN

In order to provide an accurate terrestrial backup to satellite systems such as GPS, a more accurate Enhanced LORAN (eLORAN) system is under development in Europe. Tests have shown that eLORAN will provide positional accuracy within the coverage area to the same level as GPS.

eLORAN is an internationally standardised positioning, navigation, and timing (PNT) service. It is the latest in the long-standing and proven series of low-frequency, Long-Range (LORAN) systems and takes full advantage of 21st century technology.

eLORAN is an independent, dissimilar, complement to GNSS and allows GNSS users to retain the safety, security and economic benefits of GNSS, even when their satellite services are disrupted.

As eLORAN uses high-powered transmitters and low-frequency signals (not microwatts and microwaves like GNSS), it is very unlikely to be disrupted or jammed by the same causes that would disrupt GNSS signals. Therefore low-cost, eLORAN receivers, even built into GNSS units, can mitigate the impact of disruptions to GNSS.

At sea, a new concept of navigation – enhanced navigation (e Navigation) – is being developed which requires an exceptionally reliable input of position, navigation and time data. The combination of GNSS and eLORAN has the potential to meet its needs.

Maritime users are strongly encouraged to use eLORAN as a navigational input system to back-up and complement the widespread use of GPS if the service is available.

4.4 Global Navigation Satellite System (GNSS)

When navigating in confined waters, navigators must bear in mind that the received position from any satellite positioning system is that of the antenna.

a) Global Positioning System (GPS)

GPS provides a global positioning capability giving 95% accuracy in the order of +/- 25 metres. Differential GPS (DGPS) is also available in many areas of the world including the UK coast. DGPS receivers apply instantaneous corrections (determined and transmitted by terrestrial monitoring stations) to raw GPS signals. Positional accuracy of better than 5 metres may be possible. DGPS was developed when the accuracy of commercial GPS receivers was deliberately degraded by a random error input referred to as "selective availability". Although the primary need for a differential signal correction was removed when selective availability was suspended in 2000, the DGPS function now provides a facility to independently monitor the integrity of the GPS position. Details of GPS and DGPS are given in Admiralty List of Radio Signals Volume 2.

b) Global Navigation Satellite System (GLONASS)

GLONASS is operated by the Russian Federation and available to commercial users. It is similar in concept to GPS in that it is a space-based navigation system providing a continuous world-wide position fixing system. Some receivers use both GPS and GLONASS signals to compute a more precise position. The repeatable accuracy of GLONASS is similar to GPS. Details of GLONASS are given in Admiralty List of Radio Signals Volume 2.

c) GALILEO

The European GALILEO system is still under development. This is expected to provide a world-wide position fixing capability to a similar accuracy to that of GPS and GLONASS.

4.5 GNSS – related accidents

Serious accidents have occurred because of over-reliance on satellite positioning equipment. In one case a passenger vessel grounded in clear weather because the watch-keepers had relied totally upon the GPS output which had switched to dead reckoning (DR) mode because of a detached antenna lead which was not detected by the watch-keepers. Checking the position using other means, including visual observations, would have prevented the accident.

Accidents have occurred when using a track control system linked to the GNSS. In some cases positions of aids to navigation such as buoys have been inserted as waypoints and the vessels have collided with them.

4.6 Datum and Chart Accuracy

GPS positions are referenced to the World Geodetic System 1984 Datum (WGS 84). This may not be the same as the horizontal datum of the chart in use, meaning that the position when plotted may be in error. The receiver may convert the position to other datum; however these facilities should be used with caution (see 5.6). In this case the observers must ensure that they are aware of the datum of the displayed position. Where the difference in datums is known, a note on the chart provides the offset to apply to positions referenced to WGS 84 for plotting on the chart, but where this offset is not provided, the accuracy of the plotted position should be treated with caution. DGPS positions are normally referenced to WGS 84 though regional datums, corresponding to WGS 84, may be used [e.g. North American Datum 1983 (NAD 83) in the USA] and European Terrestrial Reference System 1989 (ETRS 89).

Many areas of the world have not been surveyed to modern standards hence the positional accuracy of the charted detail on the paper chart, Raster chart or ENC may not be as accurate as the GNSS receiver derived position. Mariners should allow a sensible safety margin to account for any such discrepancies.

The prudent navigator should never rely totally on GNSS navigation and should regularly cross check the ship's position using other means particularly in areas where the charts are based on old surveys. (See also notes on use of ECDIS in section 5 below.)

Mariners must read the note on satellite-derived positions on the Admiralty charts for more information. Further information can be found in the Mariner's Handbook (NP 100) and in Annual Summary of Admiralty Notices to Mariners, No19.

Volume 2 of The Admiralty List of Radio Signals published by UKHO contains full descriptions of all GNSS systems, with notes on their correct use and limitations. Also included are descriptions and examples of over-reliance on GNSS, and a full account of the problems caused by differing horizontal datums. Mariners using satellite navigation systems are strongly advised to study the information and follow the advice contained in this publication.

5. Electronic Charts
5.1 General
There are two basic types of electronic chart systems. Those that comply with the IMO requirements for SOLAS class vessels, known as the **Electronic Chart Display and Information System (ECDIS)**, and all other types of electronic chart systems, regarded generically as **Electronic Chart Systems (ECS)**. If an ECS is carried on board, the continuous use of up-to-date paper charts remains essential for safe navigation and to fulfil carriage requirements.

To satisfy the chart carriage requirements of SOLAS Chapter V, ECDIS must use Electronic Navigational Charts ENCs. These are vector charts produced to International Hydrographic Organization standards and officially issued by or on the authority of a Government authorised Hydrographic Office or other relevant government institution. At present, ENC data is not available world-wide which limits the use of ECDIS in some areas. This situation, however, is rapidly changing and comprehensive ENC coverage of the world's major trading routes and ports is forecast to be completed before 2012.

The ENC contains all the chart information necessary for safe navigation, and may contain supplementary information in addition to that contained in the paper chart (e.g. sailing directions) which may be considered necessary for safe navigation.

ENC data must be used where it is available, but, where ENC data is not available; Raster Navigational Charts (RNC) may be used with the ECDIS in the Raster Chart Display System (RCDS) mode. However, when operating in RCDS mode, the RCDS must be used in conjunction with an appropriate folio of up-to-date paper charts.

Further guidance on the use of ECDIS with ENC or RNC data is contained in Annex 14 of the MCA SOLAS V publication and Marine Guidance Note currently MGN 285.

5.2 ENCs

The ENC is a database of individual items of digitised chart data which can be displayed as a seamless chart. ENCs of appropriate detail are provided for different navigational purposes such as coastal navigation, harbour approach and berthing. The amount of detail displayed is automatically reduced when the scale of a particular ENC is reduced, in order to lessen clutter. Individual items of data can be selected and all relevant information will be displayed (for instance, all the available information relevant to a light or navigation mark).

ENCs are therefore very much more than an electronic version of the paper chart. With vector charts the data is "layered", enabling the user to de-select certain categories of data, such as textual descriptions, which may clutter the display and may not be required at the time. It is also possible for the user to select a depth contour so providing an electronic safety contour which may automatically warn the watch-keeper when approaching shallow water. Mariners should use the facility to de-select data with extreme caution as it is possible accidentally to remove data essential for the safe navigation of the vessel.

5.3 RNCs

The Raster Chart Display System (RCDS) uses RNCs, which are exact facsimiles of official paper charts, and for which Hydrographic Offices take the same liability as for their paper products. RCDS does not have the same functionality as ECDIS. Further information on ECDIS and RCDS can be found in Annex 14 of the MCA publication "Safety of Navigation – Implementing SOLAS Chapter V 2002". This Annex also contains the text of IMO SN Circular 207 "Differences between RCDS and ECDIS"

5.4 Compliance with latest IHO Standards

ECDIS in operation comprises hardware, software and data. It is important for the safety of navigation that the application software within the ECDIS works fully in accordance with the Performance Standards and is capable of displaying all the relevant digital information contained within the ENC.

Any ECDIS which has not been upgraded to be compliant with the latest version of the ENC Product Specification or the S-52 Presentation Library may be unable to correctly display the latest charted features. Additionally the appropriate alarms and indications may not be activated even though the features have been included in the ENC. Similarly any ECDIS which is not updated to be fully compliant with the S-63 Data Protection Standards may fail to decrypt or to properly authenticate some ENCs, leading to failure to load or install.

ECDIS that is not updated for the latest version of IHO Standards may not meet the chart carriage requirements as set out in SOLAS regulation V/19.2.1.4.

The IHO Standards that relate to ECDIS, ENC production and distribution, are listed below:

IHO ECDIS Standards	Current Edition
ECDIS Display and Presentation	S-52 PresLib Edition 3.4
Electronic Navigational Chart (ENC)	S-57 Edition 3.1, S-57 Edition 3.1.1 and S-57 Maintenance Document (Cumulative) Number 8
IHO Recommended ENC Validity Checks	S-58 Edition 3.0
Raster Navigational Chart (RNC)	S-61 Edition 1.0
ENC Producer Codes	S-62 Edition 2.4
ENC Data Protection	S-63 Edition 1.1
IHO Test Data Sets for ECDIS	S-64 Edition 1.0
ENC Production Guidance	S-65 Edition 1.0

A list of all the current IHO standards is maintained within the ENC/ECDIS section of the IHO website (www.iho.int) Mariners should be aware that proper ECDIS software maintenance is an important issue and adequate measures need to be in place in accordance with the International Safety Management (ISM) Code. This may be subject to verification during Port State Control inspections.

5.5 ECDIS Alarms and Indicators
ECDIS should give alarm and or indication as per following table;

Crossing safety contour	Alarm
Area with special conditions	Alarm or Indication
Deviation from route	Alarm
Positioning system failure	Alarm
Approach to critical point	Alarm
Different geodetic datum	Alarm
IHO Test Data Sets for ECDIS	Alarm
ENC Production Guidance	Alarm
Malfunction of ECDIS	Alarm or Indication
Default safety contour	Indication
Information over scale	Indication
Large scale ENC available	Indication
Different reference system	Indication
No ENC available	Indication
Customised display	Indication
Route planning across safety contour	Indication
Route planning across specified area	Indication
Crossing a danger in route monitoring mode	Indication
System test failure	Indication

Alarm: An alarm or alarm system which announces by audible means, or audible and visual means, a condition requiring attention.

Indicator: Visual indication giving information about the condition of a system or equipment.

5.6 ECDIS Integration

Electronic chart systems are integrated with the GNSS, enabling the vessel's position to be continuously displayed. Caution should be used in areas when raster charts cannot be referenced to WGS84. Electronic charts may also be integrated with the radar and electronically plotted data from ARPA, ATA or EPA, with part or all of the radar display overlaid or under-laid on the chart display. There is a danger that the combined display may become over-cluttered with data. The overlay of target data on an electronic chart does not reduce the need for the targets to be observed on the radar display. Mariners should also exercise caution where target vectors based on the vessel's water-track are overlaid on an electronic chart which displays the vessel's ground track. (See also "Chart Radar" in paragraph 3.10 above.)

Electronic charts are becoming an essential part of the navigation system of a ship's bridge and contribute greatly to navigational safety. However they must be used prudently bearing in mind the existence of unapproved equipment and the absence of official vector data in some regions.

5.7 System based datum conversions

Manufacturers of GPS receivers, ECDIS and ECS often incorporate a user selectable datum transformation capability into their software. This capability enables users to deal with datum differences in a systematic and apparently automatic manner. Whilst this might appear to be a good thing, considerable caution needs to be exercised.

A potential problem is that a single systematic transformation is not always accurate for large regional datums. A GPS receiver position (WGS84) transformed to a regional datum by means of an average set of shifts may differ from the GPS receiver position (WGS84) amended to the regional datum by the shift note on an individual chart. The shifts provided on an individual chart are calculated specifically for the chart and the area that it covers and will be more accurate than a set of generalised shifts.

Interfacing issues might also emerge when connecting a GPS receiver to an ECDIS or ECS, particularly if the GPS receiver is configured to convert its position output to a local or regional datum. Care must be taken to ensure that GPS receivers are configured to provide position in the datum that is expected by the ECS or ECDIS. In the majority of cases this will be the WGS84 datum, but manufacturers' instructions should always be carefully consulted to ensure correct system operation.

6. Conclusion

The accuracy and functionality of electronic aids to navigation has increased considerably in recent years. However there is still a danger that over-reliance on the output from a single item of equipment may lead to an accident. The need to cross-check the vessel's position using other means is as important today as it ever was, as is the basic requirement under Rule 5 of the International Regulations for Preventing Collisions at Sea, 1972 as amended, known as COLREGS to maintain a proper lookout. Accidents have occurred with ships equipped with the best of equipment where watch-keepers have been over-reliant on the equipment output, and disaster could have been averted by the simple expedient of maintaining a proper lookout.

Further information on electronic chart systems and charts is available in 'Facts about electronic charts and carriage requirements', available for download from UKHO website (www.ukho.gov.uk).

INDEX

aground vessels, lights and shapes for 87–8
all-round lights 66
anchored vessels, lights and shapes for 87–8, 105
Annex I 103–12
Annex II 113–14
Annex III 115–18
Annex IV 119–20
attention, signals to attract 97
Automatic Identification System (AIS) 172–5
Automatic Radar Plotting Aid (ARPA) 140–1, 192–3
Automatic Tracking Aid (ATA) 192

beam, forward of the 188
bells 117–18
bicolour lights 104
breadth, definition of 18–19

channels, narrow 33–7
Chief Engineer 122
clear weather practise 195
close-quarters situations 188
closest point of approach (CPA) 188
collisions: action to avoid 29–33, 187
　　establishing a risk of collision using radar 132
　　MAIB reported collision cases 188–9
　　risk of collision 26–9, 132, 185–6
　　use of VHF to aid collision avoidance 171–2
commercial considerations 189
compliance, verification of 102
crossing situations 50–1

distress signals 97, 119–20
Dover Strait, navigation in the 176–82
dredgers, lights for 106–7

EBL, using 132–3
Electronic Chart Display and Information Systems (ECDIS) 196
　　alarms and indicators 203–4
electronic navigation aids 191–205
Electronic Navigational Charts (ENCs) 201–2
Electronic Plotting Aid (EPA) 192
Electronic Positioning Systems 199–201

Enhanced LORAN (eLORAN) 199–200
exams: preparation for 128–30
questions 142–69
exemptions 99

fishing vessels: definition of 16–17
　　lights and shapes for 77–80, 105, 106–7
　　signals for fishing vessels fishing in close proximity 113–14
　　signals for purse seiners 114
　　signals for trawlers 113–14
flashing lights 66

GALILEO 200
give-way vessels, action by 51–2
Global Navigation Satellite System (GLONASS) 200
Global Navigation Satellite System (GNSS) 200
Global Positioning System (GPS) 200
gongs 117–18
ground stabilisation 141

head-on situations 48–50
high-speed craft 112

length, definition of 18–19
lights and shapes 64–97
　　anchored vessels and vessels aground 87–8
　　colour specification of lights 108
　　exam preparation 130
　　fishing vessels 77–80
　　high-speed craft 112
　　horizontal positioning and spacing of lights 105–6
　　horizontal sectors 109–10
　　intensity of lights 109
　　intensity of non-electric lights 111
　　manoeuvring light 111
　　pilot vessels 86
　　positioning and technical details of 103–12
　　power-driven vessels underway 68–70
　　sailing vessels underway and vessels under oars 74–6
　　seaplanes 88–9
　　signals for purse seiners 114

INDEX

signals for trawlers 113–14
size of shapes 107–8
towing and pushing 70–4
vertical positioning and spacing of lights 103–5
vertical sectors 110–11
vessels constrained by their draught 85
vessels not under command or restricted in their ability to manoeuvre 80–5
visibility of lights 67–8
look-out 21–2, 122, 185
  responsibilities 124
  sole look-out 125
LORAN C 199

MAIB reported collision cases 188–9
manoeuvring: manoeuvring light 111
  manoeuvring signals 92–4
MARPA 140–1
Master 121
masthead lights 66, 105, 106
MGN 324 (M+F) Amendment 2 170–5
MGN 364 Amendment 1 176–82
MGN 369 (M+F) 182
MGN 379 (M+F) 191–205

narrow channels 33–7

oars, lights and shapes for vessels under 74–6
Officer of the Watch (OOW) 121
outlying gear, direction-indicating lights 106
overtaking 46–8

parallel index techniques 195–6
passage planning 179–81
pilot vessels, lights and shapes for 86
pilots 126–7
plotting see radar and plotting
power-driven vessels: definition of 16
  lights and shapes for 68–70
purse seiners, signals for 114
pushing, lights for 70–4

questions 142–69

radar and plotting 131–41
  ARPA and MARPA 140–1
  establishing a risk of collision using radar 132
  examples 134–40
  manual radar plotting 133
  radar and plotting aids 131–2, 192

sea and ground stabilisation 141
SOLAS regulations on radar plotting aids 131–2
Raster Navigational Charts (RNCs) 202
responsibility 13–15
  responsibilities between vessels 55–8
  watchkeeping 121
restricted visibility: conduct of vessels in 59–63, 183–5
  definition of 19
  navigation in 182–90
  sound signals in 94–7

sailing vessels: definition of 16
  lights and shapes for 74–6
  Rule 12 43–6
safe passage (impede) 42
SARTs (Search and Rescue Transponders) 198
screens for sidelights 107
sea stabilisation 141
seaplanes: definition of 17
  lights and shapes for 88–9
shapes: size 107–8
  see also lights and shapes
sidelights 66
  horizontal positioning and spacing of 105–6
  screens for 107
  vertical positioning and spacing of 104
signals: distress signals 97, 119–20
  signals for fishing vessels fishing in close proximity 113–14
  signals for purse seiners 114
  signals for trawlers 113–14
  see also lights and shapes; sound signals
SOLAS regulations on radar plotting aids 131–2
sound signals 90–7
  approval 118
  bell or gong 117–18
  distress signals 97, 119–20
  equipment for sound signals 91–2
  exam preparation 130
  manoeuvring and warning signals 92–4
  signals to attract attention 97
  sound signals in restricted visibility 94–7
  technical details of sound signal appliances 115–18
  whistles 115–17
speed, safe 22–5, 185
stand-on vessels, action by 52–5
steering and sailing rules 21–63, 183
  conduct of vessels in any condition of visibility 21–42

207

conduct of vessels in restricted visibility 59–63
conduct of vessels in sight of one another 43–58
sternlights 66

towing: towing lights 66, 70–4
    tugs and tows with long towlines 181–2
Traffic Separation Schemes (TSS) 37–42
    application of Rule 10 and navigation in the Dover Strait 176–82
    recreation activities in a UK TSS 181–2
    tugs and tows with long towlines 181–2
trawlers, signals for 113–14
tugs and tows with long towlines 181–2

underway: definition of 18
    lights and shapes for power-driven vessels underway 68–70
    lights and shapes for sailing vessels underway 74–6

vessels: definition of 16
vessels constrained by draught: definition of 18
    lights and shapes for 85, 104, 106
vessels engaged in underwater operations 106–7

vessels not under command: definition of 17
    lights and shapes for 80–5
vessels restricted in ability to manoeuvre: definition of 17–18
    lights and shapes for 80–5, 104, 106
VHF communications and usage 170–2
visibility, restricted 19
    conduct of vessels in 59–63, 183–5
    definition of 19
    navigation in 182–90
    sound signals in 94–7

warning signals 92–4
watchkeeping 121–7
    current status 123
    distractions 126
    look-out 124
    notifying the Master 127
    obligations 123
    performing the navigational watch 126
    pilots 126–7
    taking or handing over the watch 122–3
    watch arrangements and duties 122
well-run ship 189
whistles 115–17
Wing-in-Ground (WIG) 19

SOURCES

Contains public sector information licensed under the Open Government Licence v3.0.

Active Marine Guidance Notices (MGNs) have been reproduced from the Maritime and Coastguard Agency:

MGN 315: gov.uk/government/publications/mgn-315-keeping-a-safe-navigational-watch-on-merchant-vessels

MGN 324: gov.uk/government/publications/mgn-324-mf-amendment-2-navigation-watchkeeping-safety-use-of-very-high-frequency-vhf-radio-and-automatic-identification-system-ais

MGN 364: gov.uk/government/publications/mgn-364-mf-amendment-1-navigation-traffic-separation-schemes-application-of-rule-10-and-navigation-in-the-dover-strait

MGN 369: gov.uk/government/publications/mgn-369-navigation-in-restricted-visibility

MGN 379: gov.uk/government/publications/mgn-379-navigation-use-of-electronic-navigation-aids